HOW TO FOLLOW GOD'S VOICE
IN SPIRITUAL WARFARE

STUDY GUIDE

ACKNOWLEDGEMENTS

ZOE Ministries International is dedicated to training, equipping and sending believers into the world to minister by the leading of the Holy Spirit. This ministry helps build the body of Christ and encourages God's people to use their gifts and talents for His glory. It is for this purpose that this publication has been compiled by the leading of the Holy Spirit and the input of many people. ZOE Ministries wishes to thank them for their support, time, and talents in contributing to this handout packet. We give our Lord all the praise and glory for this work!

CONTENTS

HOW TO FOLLOW GOD'S VOICE—IN SPIRITUAL WARFARE
COURSE OUTLINE

Lesson 1 **INTRODUCTION**
Class Articles: *"Occupation Force,"* C. Utterbach
                         "Fascinated By God," M. Bickle

Lesson 2 **THE AUTHORITY OF THE BELIEVER**
Scripture: **Ephesians 1:1-23**
Sherman: Chapters 1 and 8
Assigned Articles: *"The Spirit Of The Word,"* J. Deere
                         "The Precious Blood Of Jesus," D. Wilkerson
                         "Reaching The Nations," E. Silvosa

Lesson 3 **WALKING IN CHRIST'S AUTHORITY**
(UNDERSTANDING WHO WE ARE)
Scripture: **Ephesians 2 and 3:14-22**
Sherman: Chapter 2
Assigned Articles: *"The Warfare Of Peace,"* J. Meyer
                         "Demons Can't Swim," D. Wilkerson

Lesson 4 **KNOWING OUR ENEMY**
Scripture: **Matthew 4:1-11; 1 Peter 5:6-11;**
                         2 Corinthians 10:3-5; Romans 12:1-2;
                         1 John 4:4; John 10:10
Sherman: Chapters 3 and 4
Assigned Articles: *"How To Silence Satan,"* T. Law
                         "Walking In The Glory," D. Wilkerson

Lesson 5 **IF THE CLOTHES FIT—WEAR THEM!**
Scripture: **Ephesians 4:17-32; 5:1-21; 6:10-18**
Renner: Chapters 1 and 2
Assigned Article: *"Exercise Your Authority,"* M. Hickey
                         "Not By The Sword Of Man," D. Wilkerson
Study Help: "If The Clothes Fit—Wear Them!" ZOE Ministries

Lesson 6 **STAYING FIT**
Scripture: **1 Samuel 17**
Sherman: Chapter 5
Renner: Chapter 3
Assigned Articles: *"Heroes Of Spiritual Warfare,"* Br. Andrew
                         "Where Evil Spirits Roam," P.Y. C
Study Help: "Who Does The Fighting?," ZOE Ministries

Lesson 7	**WARFARE IN THE HEAVENLIES**	
	Scripture:	**2 Kings 6:8-23; Daniel 10**
	Sherman:	Chapter 6
	Renner:	Chapter 4
	Assigned Articles:	*"Angels All Around,"* T. Law
		"Winning The Battle For Your Neighborhood," J. Dawson

Lesson 8	**ARE THERE SUCH THINGS AS TERRITORIAL SPIRITS?**	
	Scripture:	**2 Kings 17**
	Sherman:	Chapter 7
	Renner:	Chapter 5
	Assigned Article:	*"The Battle Is The Lord's,"* E. and A. Smith

Lesson 9	**WHY WOULD GOD ALLOW EVIL?**	
	Scripture:	**Judges 6 and 7**
	Sherman:	Chapter 9
	Assigned Articles:	*"Incense And Thunder,"* D. Hall
		"The Devil, Demons & Spiritual Warfare," J. Archer

Lesson 10	**DELIVER US FROM EVIL**	
	Scripture:	**Isaiah 58; Matthew 6:1, 16-18**
	Sherman:	Chapter 10
	Assigned Articles:	*"Guidelines For Fasting,"* P. Smith
		"The Devil's Deadline!," D. Wilkerson
	Study Help:	"The Importance Of Fasting," ZOE Ministries

Lesson 11	**KEYS OF THE KINGDOM**	
	Scripture:	**Matthew 16:13-19; 18:18-20**
	Sherman:	Chapter 11
	Assigned Article:	*"Tearing Down Strongholds Through Praise,"* C. Jacobs

Lesson 12	**VICTORY**	
	Scripture:	**2 Chronicles 20:1-30; Mark 16:14-20**
	Sherman:	Chapter 12
	Assigned Articles:	*"Spiritual Warfare Through Worship,"* G. Mira
		"The Upper Room Perfume," S. Hagan

Study Materials:

1. Bible, any version
2. Dean Sherman, *Spiritual Warfare For Every Christian*, YWAM Publishing, Seattle, Washington, 1990
3. Rick Renner, *Spiritual Weapons To Defeat The Enemy*, Pillar Book & Publishing Company, Tulsa, Oklahoma, 1991.
4. Various articles:
   a. Class Articles—to be read in class.
   b. Assigned Articles—to be read in preparation for class.
   c. Study Help— for the student's use in studying Scripture.

Dear Participant,

Praise the Lord for leading you to take this How to Follow God's Voice - In Spiritual Warfare course. We are excited about the lives that have been radically changed and empowered for God's purposes!

When we began assembling this course, there were so many different directions we could have taken. Many great men and women have written profound thoughts about this subject. However, the Holy Spirit was quite direct about setting down the principles of "knowing who we are in Christ Jesus." All warfare prayer will be ineffective if we don't know and recognize our position and authority in Christ Jesus. **"Praise be to the God and Father of our Lord Jesus Christ, who has blessed us in the heavenly realms with every spiritual blessing in Christ... And God raised us up with Christ and seated us with him in the heavenly realms with Christ Jesus..."** Ephesians 1:3; 2:6.

Just as Jesus acknowledged the works of the enemy, we, too, need to acknowledge that reality. However, we must keep in perspective that **"greater is he that is in us than he that is in the world"** 1 John 4:4 (KJV). We must at all times keep our hearts focused on the works of Jesus and the Holy Spirit.

These 12 weeks will truly offer an exciting time of seeking the Lord's direction for different areas in your life. So, enjoy the course and watch God move.

May God bless you abundantly.

Dick and Ginny Chanda
Founding Directors
ZOE Ministries International

A NOTE TO COURSE PARTICIPANTS

What ZOE Is!

1. A ministry that provides training for disciple-making.
2. Participatory classes where all are encouraged to share and contribute.
3. A situation where the leader (facilitator) decreases and the participants increase.
4. A drawing out of ministry gifts and preparation for the Lord's calling on individual lives.
5. A time when one can grow in the understanding and appreciation of others' gifts.
6. A safe environment in which an individual can feel comfortable to practice operating in his or her gifts.
7. A time of understanding the heart of the Father and applying that to one's life.

What ZOE Is Not!

1. A traditional Bible study.
2. A course where the leader speaks and the people take notes.
3. A place where people can air their opinions or gripes.
4. A place where people can discuss church doctrines.
5. A time when "weird" ministry happens.

A Reminder to Participants:

"A ZOE class is not just a Bible study; our leader is a facilitator and coach, not a teacher."

It is our desire that the Lord Jesus Christ be glorified in all that is said and done in ZOE classes. We wish to foster an understanding of the operation of His Holy Spirit and to yield to His workings.

MAIN PRINCIPLES

Lesson 1: We do not focus on Satan or glorify him in any way. However, we do acknowledge his existence for the purpose of strengthening our capabilities in dealing with him in spiritual warfare. Our God is a mighty, all-powerful God—a victorious and undefeatable Lord!

Lesson 2: We are adopted children of God and have been redeemed by the blood of Jesus. As we live holy lives in submission to God, we can walk in Jesus' power and authority. In Christ we have been given spiritual blessings that give us victory over the enemy.

Lesson 3: Are we a victim or a victor? Spiritual warfare does not come with an option. As soon as we accept Jesus, we have joined His forces. However, when we understand the authority the Lord has given us and our identity in Christ, we will become victorious.

Lesson 4: Just to recognize the enemy is not enough. We also need to know what he is capable of and where he stands in comparison to God.

Lesson 5: God has equipped us with spiritual armor. With the full armor of God, we are fully prepared to stand against the enemy.

Lesson 6: In Christ, we are strong. We need to keep our strength by maintaining our relationship with God through prayer, meditation on Scripture, worship and fellowship. As we learn to recognize the schemes of Satan, we will become proficient at resisting them in the power of the Spirit.

Lesson 7: We are seated with Christ in heavenly places far above all rule and authority, power and dominion. God has given us the ministry of angels to help and protect us. In prayer, we can appropriate their help in the spiritual realm to accomplish what God has called us to do.

Lesson 8: The very definition of principalities tells us that we are dealing with spirits that operate both demographically and geographically. Yet, the Church has paid little or no attention to territorial spirits! We need to ask the Holy Spirit to sharpen our ability to discern and identify such spirits so that we pray more effectively.

Lesson 9: God gets blamed for everything! Do we blame God for the problems in our lives? Do we turn to God only when there is a problem? God doesn't create evil, but He does use it to cause us to grow more in His likeness.

Lesson 10: We see from our Lord's example that fasting does not change our position with God; it intensifies the power released toward satanic strongholds. Fasting should be a lifestyle!

Lesson 11: Is our prayer life self-centered or does it reflect God's heart? Prayer does change things. It can have an impact on our lives, families, cities, countries and other nations. We need to pray God's heart in all areas of our lives.

Lesson 12: If we plan to be used by God to advance His kingdom, we will definitely feel the enemy's resistance. However, we have been given offensive weapons that counteract the tactics of the enemy. We will see victory when we remember that "spiritual warfare is not just a prayer prayed or a demon rebuked—it is a life lived."

PARTICIPANT'S RESPONSIBILITIES

I. Class Preparation

A. Read the assigned scriptures and come prepared to share in class.

1. Ask the Holy Spirit, **"Open my eyes that I may see wonderful things in Your law."** **Psalm 119:18** You may be very familiar with the assigned Scriptures, but the Lord is very faithful and can give you "fresh manna."

2. Look at the Main Principle for the lesson and apply the Scriptures. Ask yourself the following questions:
   a. How does this Scripture apply to the lesson?
   b. How does this Scripture apply to my life?
   c. What do I need to do to apply this Scripture to my life and to the lives of others for God's glory?

B. Read the assigned chapters or pages in the book and come prepared to share in the class.
Note in your book any thoughts related to the Main Principle for the lesson.

C. Read the assigned articles and come prepared to share in the class.
Note any thoughts related to the Main Principle for the lesson.

D. Maintain a journal—a valuable tool in God's hands.
As you learn to hear God's voice and keep a record of His speaking, you will become more aware of what He is saying to you and how He wants to work through you. See the article "Journaling—A Good Way to Hear God's Voice."

E. Spend time in prayer.
1. Prayer is valuable preparation for these classes. The more time you spend with the Lord, the more you will come to know Him.
2. Spend time with God daily! Avoid crash studying. God shows no partiality—what He has done for others, He will do for you! Growth will come as you respond to God's Holy Spirit at work in your life.

II. Class Participation

A. Training is active! You will be encouraged to **take part in the class discussions and the prayer and ministry time.**

B. You will have the opportunity to **lead the discussion** of the assigned reading as you feel comfortable. No one will be forced to lead—only encouraged! Discussion Leader assignments are made two weeks in advance so that you have ample time to prepare. There is a helpful handout on leading class discussions in your Study Guide.

JOURNALING – A GOOD WAY TO HEAR GOD'S VOICE

What Goes Into a Journal?

1. Your thoughts—impressions, insights, hopes, fears, goals, struggles.
2. Your feelings—both positive and negative.
3. Your prayers and answers to prayer.
4. Excerpts from Scripture and other reading that God seems to be highlighting for you.

How to Journal

1. You may choose to use a spiral binder or a hardback blank book, or anything that you can take with you easily on trips.
2. Journal every day, if possible, during the time that you read Scripture and pray. Record in it insights that the Lord gave you that day or the day before.
3. You may want to keep a separate section in your journal for prayers or excerpts from your reading.
4. Write directly to God as if you were talking to Him or writing Him a letter.

The Benefits of Keeping a Journal are Many

1. Journaling fosters a readiness to hear from God. Personal communion with God takes place as you write out your thoughts and feelings, and record the insights and impressions He gives you.
2. As you read God's Word and record your insights about Scripture, God is faithful to provide the admonitions, encouragement and guidance that you need.
3. Prayers become specific as you place them in print. In addition, God gets the glory when you review your journal and see your prayers have been answered.
4. Journaling helps clarify your thinking. Fears and struggles are more clearly defined so that they can be dealt with.
5. During times of discouragement, it can help to look back over your journal and see God's faithfulness and your progress in spiritual growth.

GUIDELINES FOR LEADING A COURSE DISCUSSION

1. Prayer

As you study the assigned material, ask God for insights. Ask Him to show you the main points to be discussed and questions to ask to aid the discussion. Come a few minutes early to the class and pray with the Facilitators before the class begins.

2. Maintain Control of the Discussion

After the class has been turned over to you by the Facilitators, you are to maintain control of the discussion.

   a. Do not allow one or two participants to dominate the discussion time.

   b. Stick to the subject. God may give you many insights, but keep the discussion related to the Main Principle of the lesson.

3. Work Within the Allotted Time

For a 2½ hour course:

   Approximately 30 minutes for the book

   Approximately 50 minutes for the Scripture discussion

   Approximately 15 minutes for the articles

     (Allowing 20 min. for the Facilitators to lead the prayer/ministry)

For a 1½ hour course:

   Approximately 20 minutes for the book

   Approximately 30 minutes for the Scripture discussion

   Approximately 10 minutes for the articles

     (Allowing 10 min. for the Facilitators to lead the prayer/ministry)

ZOE courses focus on what God says through the Bible. Be careful not to spend too much time on the book or articles, which are provided only as supplements to the Scriptures.

4. Encourage Discussion

Course members should be prepared to share insights that the Lord gave them while they read the assigned material. You may need to draw out these insights by asking questions.

   a. Begin with a *launch* question, a broad question that can be answered in a number of different ways by anyone in the group.

   b. Then use *guide* questions, which are short questions that keep the discussion moving in a direction that is related to the Main Principle of that lesson. Life application of the principles found in the assigned reading should be a focus during some part of the discussion.

   c. To close the discussion time, summarize very briefly the main points of the discussion.

May God bless you as you study and pray in preparation for the course. We will be praying for you as you prepare. We love and appreciate you. ~ *The Facilitators*

LESSON 1

INTRODUCTION

MAIN PRINCIPLE

*We do not focus on Satan or glorify him in any way.
However, we do acknowledge his existence for the purpose
of strengthening our capabilities in dealing with him in
spiritual warfare. Our God is a mighty, all-powerful God—a
victorious and undefeatable Lord!*

DISCLAIMER

The articles that follow have been chosen to give you, the reader, a broader perspective on many of the issues presented in the course. All the ideas in these articles do not necessarily represent the views of *ZOE Ministries International*. However, we pray that as you read and study, you will glean a sense of what is in the author's heart. At all times we need to ask the question, "Does this line up with the Word of God?"

CLASS ARTICLE

OCCUPATION FORCE

by Clinton Utterbach

Matthew 11:12 says, *"From the days of John the Baptist until now the kingdom of heaven suffers violence, and the violent take it by force."* The Bible also tells us that we are not fighting against flesh and blood, but against principalities and powers (Eph. 6:12).

In this battle, God has not called us to fight in our own strength. The Holy Spirit is called alongside to help us, and He will supply the power. Reaching the world seems like an overwhelming task. But if we prayerfully do as much as we're able to, God will do the rest.

In every military campaign, the army that emerges victoriously must eventually occupy the territory of the defeated foe. On D-Day, the American forces invaded Europe. We had to actually go and take over the territory of Hitler's Germany. We couldn't just stay on this side of the Atlantic and hope everything would turn out fine. We had to go to where the enemy was and fight. The superior might has to bring the enemy to a place of surrender. It's no different in spiritual warfare.

We need to be willing to do whatever God has authorized and commanded us to do at any given time. The most important lesson I have learned in studying the Word of God is how to be led by the Spirit of God. The Bible tells us that any-body who is a child of God is led by His Spirit. This means that the work the Holy Spirit leads me to do might be different from the work He leads another to do. We are all one body, but we are different members called to do different things. We have to know what we've been called to do.

Nobody ever occupied the territory of the enemy without a fight, and the devil is certainly not going to surrender his territory without a fight. Only by spiritual force can we occupy territory that has been the devil's stronghold in our life or in the lives of others.

...WE ARE THE ONES WHO ARE RECLAIMING THE AREA OF THE ENEMY.

When we go into the battle to which we've been assigned, we have to be equipped with the power of Almighty God. There's nothing more important than knowing that the Holy Spirit in us is greater than any spirit or force we will encounter. We are the occupying force; we are the ones who are reclaiming the area of the enemy.

Jesus said the very gates of hell would not prevail against the Church (Matt. 16:18). When I was growing up, the Church had a defensive attitude. We thought the Church was this great fortress and the devil was bombarding the doors of that fortress. We weren't going to let him in.

But the Church is called to be more than defensive; we are to occupy by powerful force. And the devil's gates will not be able to prevail against us *as we do what God has commanded us to do*. We have to go with confidence and faith, understanding that the battle really is not ours; it's God's. Our warfare is in the spirit realm.

We are to put on the whole armor of God. The helmet of salvation is stronger than a physical helmet. The spiritual breastplate of righteousness is more powerful than a physical one. We need to be girded with truth and our feed shod with the preparation of the Gospel of peace. We need to take the sword of the spirit – the Word of God. Above all, we must take the shield of faith, which can quench the fiery darts of the enemy (Eph. 6:11-17).

The Bible says the violent take the kingdom by force, spiritual force. For years, Christians thought that Canaan was a type of heaven. But it could not possibly be heaven because we won't have any enemies there. When Israel got to Canaan, they had all kinds of mortal enemies. In order to inhabit the land, they were required to take it from the enemy.

Canaan is a type of the believer's walk in the Spirit. As we walk in the Spirit every day, we encounter all kinds of enemies – natural and spiritual. The way we become victorious is to know what kind of spiritual arsenal we should use.

When we're dealing with people, it's easy to blame them for doing something when actually there's a spiritual force motivating them. We have to make this distinction and love people but come against the force that's motivating them. We need to show them the love God has for the world. We'll have to pray for those who are being used by the adversary.

We have to put the Word into practice. When we are born again, spiritual forces are deposited into our spirits: love, joy, peace, longsuffering, kindness, goodness and faithfulness. God has deposited His power in believers. The fruit of the Spirit is for personal character, while the gifts of the Spirit are for power to help others.

We must go in the power of the Holy Spirit and occupy the enemy's territory. *"But you shall receive power when the Holy Spirit has come upon you; and you shall be witnesses to Me in Jerusalem* (where they were), *and in all Judea* (the surrounding area), *and Samaria* (where they never wanted to go as Jews), *and to the end of the earth* (where they had never been)" (Acts 1:8). We are equipped first to minister where we are (perhaps to family and friends), then in the surrounding community and in places we have never been. God will energize us to do that.

Numbers 13:17-19 says, *"Then Moses sent them to spy out the land of Canaan, and said to them, 'Go up this way into the South, and go up to the mountains, and see what the land is like: whether the people who dwell in it are strong or weak, few or many; whether the land they dwell in is good or bad; whether the cities they inhabit are like camps or strongholds.'"*

Notice the directive was to go and find out what were the strengths and weaknesses of the enemy. God never told Moses to do anything except send the people in there to see what the land was like and to determine the strengths and weaknesses of the enemy. But He told them beforehand: "I am giving you the land."

When the spies returned to Moses, they reported: *"'We went to the land where you sent us. It truly flows with milk and honey, and this is its fruit. Nevertheless the people who dwell in the land are strong; the cities are fortified and very large; moreover we saw the descendants of Anak there.' … Then Caleb quieted the people before Moses, and said, 'Let us go up at once and take possession for we are well able to overcome it'"* (Num. 13:27,28,30).

IF GOD IS GOING TO GIVE US SOMETHING, IT DOESN'T MATTER WHO'S THERE OR WHAT IT LOOKS LIKE.

We must have Caleb's attitude no matter what the circumstances look like. If God tells us to go, we have to say, "Let us go at once." If we don't go at once, the devil will begin to talk us out of it. God told Moses that He was going to give them the land. So it didn't really matter whether the people were strong or weak.

If God is going to give us something, it doesn't matter who's there or what it looks like. When we were trying to get our church building, it looked like it was an impossibility with the size of the congregation and the amount of money we had. But God had already promised us that the money would come.

God told my wife to go and speak to the building. So she would drive around the building in the morning, roll down the window in the parking lot, and look at this empty facility and say, "You will not function anymore except as the Redeeming Love Christian Center." She did that day after day.

After two-and-a-half years, the corporation that owned the building called us back and asked us if we wanted it. They couldn't use it as a theater because the town had voted against it. In the interim, God had increased our congregation from 300 members with $250,000 in the bank to 900 members with $1.6 million in the bank. We were well able to possess it.

Every delay is not a defeat. Sometimes God has to delay things in order to get us ready. Sometimes He has to delay things to line up necessary circumstances. But when God puts a vision or a dream in a person's heart, He is committed to bring it to pass. He only requires that we stay steady and wait for the vision.

The Lord quickened this Scripture to my wife some years ago, and we put it on the walls of the church: *"The vision is yet for an appointed time; but at the end it will speak, and it will not lie. Though it tarries, wait for it; because it will surely come, it will not tarry"* (Hab. 2:3). If God has given us a vision or a dream and told us to do something, it is for an appointed time. Even Jesus did not come until the fullness of time had come.

"We are not able to go up against the people, for they are stronger than we" (Num. 13:31). That was a declaration of doubt. But *"let us go up at once and take possession, for we are well able to*

overcome it" (Num. 13:30) is the covenant declaration.

That's my heart's cry. I have taught prosperity and had prosperity. God has proven to me that He will meet my every need, and I don't need to quote a lot of prosperity Scriptures. All I need to do is seek first the kingdom of God and His righteousness and these things will start to be added unto me.

I look over my right shoulder and goodness is following me. I look over my left shoulder and mercy is following me. I've walked through the valley of the shadow of death with a dissecting aneurism doctors said was 99% fatal without an operation. I didn't have an operation. That was 1979 and I'm still here.

I desire to see people in darkness come to the light. I desire to see people translated out of darkness and into the kingdom of the Son of God's love. I won't be satisfied until God moves in this earth in a magnificent way.

We are the tools He is going to use. We have to be willing to go into the enemy's territory and know that when we get there, God will show up. Sometimes we just have to be somewhere. When we show up, God will show up. We are vessels filled with Almighty God, going somewhere to do His bidding. Let's always remember to be obedient to the leading of the Spirit, and God will support what He has authorized.

——Adapted from a message given at CFNI in Dallas.

Clinton Utterbach died in 2007. He was formerly a choir director and composer, then later a pastor and preacher of Redeeming Love Christian Center in Nanuet, New York.

Reprinted by permission: Christ for the Nations CFNI, P.O. Box 769000, Dallas, TX 75376-9000, 800-933-2364

FASCINATED BY GOD
Passion for Jesus

by Mike Bickle

We all know that it takes God to love God. The human heart does not have the capacity to generate holy love in its own power. However, there is good news for those already born again what the Holy Spirit enjoys most and does best is to escort the heart of the spiritually hungry into a realm of experiential knowledge of the splendor of Jesus. This new knowledge leaves us fascinated and exhilarated.

How does this work? It begins with the way God originally designed the human spirit. A fascinating God created us with a deep longing to be fascinated. The entertainment industry has built its entire business on this craving.

LIVING WITH OUR HEARTS FASCINATED BY GOD'S AFFECTION IS THE FOUNTAINHEAD OF RENEWAL.

But God intended for us to be fascinated only by Him. We must learn how to satisfy our craving in Him instead of in ungodly ways.

If we don't, we will live bored. Spiritual boredom is one of the greatest problems in the church today. Such boredom makes us more vulnerable to Satan's attacks.

We were never designed to live bored. If we have nothing to die for, then we have nothing to live for. We are meant to live in full vigor and abandonment. In this way, the designs of our hearts can be fully answered.

The supernatural ability to love God with fiery and energetic affections is the privilege of every believer. It is the very essence of New Testament renewal as preached by the apostle Paul. He exhorted the Colossian church to "put on the new man who is renewed in knowledge according to the image of Him" (Col. 3:10, NKJV).

Notice that Paul taught the church to put on the new man by experiencing the knowledge of God's image, or personality. This knowledge fascinates and renews us so that we can live in the abandonment to God that our human design demands.

Supernatural information about God's emotional makeup has a surprisingly powerful impact on our emotional chemistry. Knowledge of God actually releases God's power in us. Living with our hearts fascinated by fresh discoveries of God's affection and beauty is the fountainhead of renewal.

Paul beckons us all to experience renewal of the heart that results in a dynamic emotional chemistry change. Knowing god's beauty fascinates and awakens our hearts in a supernatural way. Oh, to know what God's heart looks like, and to know what we look like to God in Jesus! This revelation results in true transformation. that He promised.

How do we get it? The revelation comes as we meditate on passages in the Word of God that focus on God's personality or splendor. The Holy Spirit then illuminates our minds, and a place deep within us says, "Yes, that is true." Our spirits begin to resonate with the very flame of the love of God, and we are empowered for righteousness and fulfilling the Great Commission.

December 1999, Charisma

Oh, to live fascinated! When we do, we desire worship, we desire the Word of God, and obedience seems reasonable.

As we gain ever-increasing knowledge of God along with greater knowledge of who we are in Christ, we experience an internal change that deeply motivates us in righteousness. Satan knows that when we walk in a revelatory understanding of what God looks like and what we look like to God, his power of accusation is broken. We truly are renewed according to our knowledge of the image of God.

When people ask me, based on a book I wrote, how to grow in passion for Jesus, I tell them to grow in knowledge of *His* passion for *them*, and over time they will see the passions of their hearts awaken with deep, affectionate love for Him. Because of the way our hearts have been designed and created by God, when we receive greater revelation of Him we are renewed, invigorated and emotionally empowered. The more we see of His fascinating beauty, the more we are awakened in love.

We must see the intensity with which God desires us! We are the very focus of His burning desire. He enjoys us. He is ravished by us. When we lay hold of this revelation, we will never be the same.

—Mike Bickle is an author and the director of the International House of Prayer Missions Base of Kansas City (IHOP–KC), an organization based on 24/7 prayer with worship that is engaged in inner city outreaches along with justice initiatives, planting houses of prayer, and training missionaries.

LESSON 2

THE AUTHORITY OF THE BELIEVER

MAIN PRINCIPLE

We are adopted children of God and have been redeemed by the blood of Jesus. As we live holy lives in submission to God, we can walk in Jesus' power and authority. In Christ we have been given spiritual blessings that give us victory over the enemy.

ASSIGNED ARTICLE

THE SPIRIT OF THE WORD

by Jack Deere

THOSE OF US WHO ARE CHARISMATIC NEED TO REMEMBER THAT THE MOST IMPORTANT WAY GOD SPEAKS TO US IS THROUGH SCRIPTURES.

The only person Monica loved more than her son was her God, the Lord Jesus Christ. When her son was a baby, she would sing hymns while nursing him. She dedicated him to the Lord and prayed he would be a blessing to the kingdom of God.

Monica's faith and love were well-known throughout the Christian community in her city, and when her son grew up, his brilliance was equally well-known. But so was his immorality and hostility toward God.

The young man had become a rhetoric professor. He had given himself over to the full-time occupation of drunkenness, sexual immorality and turning people away from the one, true God with his philosophical speculations. Even the most highly trained Christian intellectuals could make no headway with Monica's son.

Monica came close to utter despair several times but refused to give up. She continued to labor in prayer for the salvation of her son. When he was 19 years old, Monica had a dream. In this dream she and her son were walking in heaven, hand in hand.

She knew God was telling her through the dream that He would save her immoral son. It encouraged Monica to intensify her prayers. A year went by. Then another year. And another. Instead of her son growing closer to God, he seemed to be growing further away. He was now more intelligent, more arrogant and more committed to evil than ever before.

A famous, respected and wise church leader visited Monica's city to conduct some religious services. Because Monica was so highly thought of, it was not difficult for her to obtain a private meeting with the leader.

She told him of her prayers for her son and that his condition had actually worsened. She implored the leader to speak with her son, but he refused. He knew any attempt on his part to persuade Monica's son to repent would only serve to harden his heart.

"How will my son ever be saved?" Monica sobbed. The wise old man looked down on Monica's tear-stained face with affection.

"Woman," he said, "it is impossible for the son of those tears to perish." Their meeting was over.

Monica, encouraged by his words the same way she had been encouraged by her dream years earlier, continued to do the only thing she could do--pray, this time with a renewed zeal.

Nine years after Monica's dream, her son was sitting in a garden, still an unbeliever, when he heard an audible voice speak the words, "Take it and read, take it and read...," over and over in the singsong voice of a child's nursery song. At first he thought there were children playing nearby. But there were no children, and it was a song he had never heard before. He sensed the voice was a divine command from heaven to open the Scriptures and read.

Monica's son took up the Bible, and his eyes fell on Romans 13:13-14: "Let us walk decently, as in the daytime, not in orgies and drunkenness, not in sexual immorality and debauchery, not in dissension and jealousy. Rather, clothe yourselves with the Lord Jesus Christ, and do not think about how to gratify the desires of the sinful nature" (NIV).

The son's heart was miraculously transformed. He would no longer be known as Monica's immoral son. Instead, he would go down in history as St. Augustine – one of the greatest theologians and champions of the faith in the entire history of the church.

A few years after Augustine had been saved, Monica said to him: "My son, for my part I find no further pleasure in this life. What I am still to do or why I am here in the world, I do not know, for I have no more hope on this earth." She had been given the great desire of her heart, her son's salvation. There was nothing more she wanted in this life. Nine days later she died.

THE POWER OF THE BIBLE

When Monica came close to despair, God gave her a dream to encourage her to keep praying. When she came to another low point, He gave her a prophetic word from a bishop of the church. And when the time was right in His eyes, God the Father sent His audible voice to the rebellious Augustine and opened his heart through the words of Scripture.

In the fourth century God was still speaking through dreams, prophetic words, His audible voice and Scripture. You might be tempted to think the written Word of God wouldn't be necessary in the presence of dreams, prophetic words and an audible voice. But in Augustine's case the voice was meant to lead him to that passage in Romans, which God illuminated

in such a way to lead him to a new birth in Christ.

When the Bible is illuminated by the Holy Spirit, its power is incredible. Its light can dispel the darkness of the most convincing satanic deception. Many since Augustine have been surprised by the power of God's Word.

Dorothy is a woman I know who was sinking into suicidal despair. She came to church on Easter Sunday hoping to find an excuse not to take her life. She listened to a sermon on Luke 24, but nothing about it gave her any hope. That night she stood in front of her mirror to say goodbye to a life filled with suffering and despair.

As she prepared to commit suicide, a text of Scripture from the morning's sermon rose up in her heart–" 'Did not the Christ have to suffer these things and then enter His glory?' " (Luke 24:26). That was it! First the suffering, then the glory. If she ended her suffering by her own hand, she might miss the glory later. If Christ suffered before He came into His glory, then so would she.

Dorothy put down the pills and picked up her Bible, The voice of God not only surprised her, but it completely drowned out the demonic voice asking for her life.

///

"THE ONLY ONES WHO WILL SUCCESSFULLY PERSEVERE THROUGH TRIALS ARE THOSE WHO LOVE THE WORD OF GOD."

///

Such is the power of God's written Word, and such is God's commitment to use it in our lives. The one who heard the Father's voice better than anyone said, " 'I tell you the truth, until heaven and earth disappear, not the smallest letter, not the least stroke of a pen, will by any means disappear from the Law until everything is accomplished' " (Matt. 5:18). Anyone who ignores the Bible is inviting deception and disaster to be their intimate companions in the journey of life.

BENEFITS FROM THE BIBLE

The most common way the Holy Spirit reveals Jesus and speaks to us today is through the Bible. No one has ever said it better than the apostle Paul: "All Scripture is God-breathed and is useful for teaching, rebuking, correcting and training in righteousness, so that the man of God may be thoroughly equipped for every good work" (2 Tim. 3:16-17).

No one has ever illustrated this truth better than Jesus did on the road to Emmaus (see Luke 24:13-23). After Jesus' death, the disciples were tremendously depressed. At one time they had been confident that He was the Redeemer of Israel, but by this time they had lost that confidence. Jesus had predicted His death and resurrection on several occasions. He had told the disciples He would rise from the grave after three days (see Luke 9:22, John 2:19).

Now it was the third day, and the tomb was empty. They had even heard a report from the women who had visited the tomb-angels telling them that Jesus was alive. Still, in spite of all these positive indications, the disciples could not get back their confidence in Jesus.

January/February 1999, Ministry Today

When Jesus appeared to the two disciples as they were walking along the Emmaus road, they did not recognize Him. He listened to their tale of woe up until the point where they mentioned the empty tomb. Then He said to them: " 'How foolish you are, and how slow of heart to believe all that the prophets have spoken! Did not the Christ have to suffer these things and then enter His glory?' " (Luke 24:25-26).

At this point, you would think Jesus would simply reveal Himself so they could believe in His resurrection. Instead of doing that, He preached a sermon to them--"beginning with Moses and all the prophets, He explained to them what was said in all the Scriptures concerning Himself" (Luke 24:27).

Here was the greatest sermon of all time, preached by Jesus on the first resurrection morning. The theme was Jesus, the text was Moses and all the prophets, and only two people were in the audience! It went on for hours. Think of it--the greatest sermon ever preached was preached by Jesus to only two people.

Why didn't Jesus simply reveal Himself to the disciples at the beginning of their walk? Why did He take them to the Scriptures? Jesus was telling us, right at the very beginning of the church's history, that the primary way He will be known is through Scripture. This is the primary benefit of the Bible--it reveals Jesus to us.

GUIDANCE AND THE BIBLE

Turning to the book of Acts, we find that the apostles showed the same respect as Jesus did for the Bible. We would expect them to use the Scripture to prove the basic truths of the gospel, and they do. For example, Paul used Psalm 2:7, Isaiah 55:3 and Psalm 16:10 to prove God raised Jesus from the dead (see Acts 13:32-35).

God used the Bible to do more than teach theological truths. He used it to guide His servants in ministry. The Holy Spirit illuminated Psalm 69:25 and Psalm 109:8 to show Peter that He wanted to choose another apostle to fill the vacancy left by Judas (see Acts 1:15-22).

God also used the Bible to explain circumstances and events in the life of the early church. When the Holy Spirit brought the mighty wind and tongues of fire on Pentecost, many people thought those in the Upper Room were drunk. But God opened Peter's mind to understand that these phenomena were the beginning of a fulfillment of the ancient prophecy spoken of in Joel 2:28-32. Peter used that passage to explain to the crowd the meaning of Pentecost (see Acts 2:14-21).

OBEDIENCE AND THE BIBLE

Neither Jesus nor the apostles were the least bit innovative in their attitude toward the Scriptures. The people of God, especially God's leaders, had always shared a respect for the authority and power of God's holy, written Word. When Moses passed from the scene and the leadership of God's people fell to Joshua, God gave Joshua one of the most extraordinary promises ever given to an individual. He said to him: " 'No one will be able to stand up against you all the days of your life. As I was with Moses, so I will be with you; I will never leave you nor forsake you' " (Josh. 1:5).

With this promise, Joshua was virtually assured a success and a protection very few world leaders have ever enjoyed. Yet Joshua was very apprehensive about trying to fill Moses' place. Three times during his commissioning service the Lord had to warn him to be "strong and courageous" (Josh. 1:6-9). After all, who could really take the place of Moses? Who would want to! Moses had been given the impossible task of leading a people who had been rebellious to God throughout the tenure of his entire leadership (see Deut. 9:24).

Moses himself had not been permitted to go into the promised land. How would Joshua ever take them in?

The secret of Joshua's future success was not found in his leadership skills or his discipline, but in the first person singular pronoun "I." God promised: "I will be with you; I will never leave you nor forsake you." When spoken by God, there is no more powerful force on earth than this pronoun. God made a commitment to prosper Joshua. That was the divine part.

Now for the human part. Joshua had one main responsibility in order to fully enjoy the promise of God's commitment. God commanded Joshua: " 'Be strong and very courageous. Be careful to obey all the law my servant Moses gave you; do not turn from it to the right or to the left, that you may be successful wherever you go. Do not let this Book of the Law depart from your mouth; meditate on it day and night, so that you may be careful to do everything written in it. Then you will be prosperous and successful' " (Josh. 1:7-8).

At first this command to meditate on the Scriptures day and night doesn't seem to make much sense. Joshua knew the Law better than any living Israelite. He probably acted as Moses' scribe on a number of occasions when Scripture was actually being written. He had spent 40 years serving the man of God and studying the words of God. You would think that by now he knew the Bible so well, he could relax a little. Why should he have to meditate on it day and night at this stage of his life?

The answer is this. There is a realm of obedience that requires us to be careful to do everything written in God's Word (see Josh. 1:8). The only people who will ever enter that realm of obedience are those that meditate on the Law day and night. The only people who will ever have the divine success the Lord wishes to give them in this life are those who meditate day and night on His holy Word. And the greater the responsibility God gives to individuals in His kingdom, the greater their need to meditate on His Word.

STABILITY AND THE BIBLE

The only people who achieve real stability in their inner lives are the people who meditate day and night on the law of the Lord. The person who does that "is like a tree planted by streams of water, which yields its fruit in season and whose leaf does not wither. Whatever he does prospers" (Ps. 1:3). The only people who are successful at
resisting lust, greed and temptation are the ones who treasure the Word of God in their hearts (see Ps. 119:9-11).

The only ones who will successfully persevere through trials are those who love the Word of God. The psalmist said, "If your law had not been my delight, I would have perished in my affliction" (Ps. 119:92). The same psalmist reminds us that, "Great peace have they who love your law, and nothing can make them stumble" (Ps. 119:165). All these benefits and more are given by the Holy Spirit to the person who consistently visits the Word of God with a pure heart.

No one said it better than the psalmist:

The law of the Lord is perfect,
reviving the soul.
The statutes of the Lord are trustworthy,
Making wise the simple.
The precepts of the Lord are right,
giving joy to the heart.
The commands of the Lord are radiant,
giving light to the eyes.
The fear of the Lord is pure,
enduring forever.
The ordinances of the Lord are sure
and altogether righteous.
They are more precious than gold,
than much pure gold;
They are sweeter than honey,
than honey from the comb.
By them is your servant warned;
in keeping them there is great reward
(Ps. 19:7-11).

There is no book like the Bible and no substitute for consistent daily meditation in the Scriptures. The Holy Spirit is committed to nourishing and washing our hearts by the words of the Bible.

— Jack Deere has many years of pastoral experience and is currently senior pastor of the Wellspring Church in Ft. Worth, Texas, a church he started in the spring of 2004. He also served as Dean of the Wagner Leadership Institute in Colorado Springs, Colorado.

THE PRECIOUS BLOOD OF JESUS!

by David Wilkerson

Without a doubt, the blood of Jesus Christ is the most precious gift our heavenly Father has given to His church. Yet so few Christians understand its value and virtue.

Christians often sing about the power of the blood. Indeed, the anthem of the Pentecostal church is, "There is power, power, wonder-working power in the precious blood of the Lamb." But most believers seldom enter into the power of that blood.

We simply do not comprehend the great significance of the blood. For example: We constantly "plead the blood" as some kind of mystical formula of protection. But few Christians can explain its great glory and benefits.

If I were to ask you what the power of the blood means, you might answer, "It means that my sins are remitted—that I'm free from the bondage of iniquity -- that all my sins are covered." Yet, beyond forgiveness, what does the blood of Jesus Christ mean to you? Can you explain to me, to your family, to a coworker the value and virtue of the blood of Jesus?

I want to give you a fuller understanding of the preciousness of Jesus' blood—and how it can work wonderful changes in your life!

1. In Scripture the Blood Is Spoken of in Two Ways — Blood Shed and Blood Sprinkled!

Most Christians know about the blood Jesus shed for us. When Christ lifted the cup at the last Passover, He said, "...This cup is the new testament in my blood, which is shed for you" (Luke 22:20).

We memorialize His sacrifice every time we have communion. But that is the limit of most Christians' knowledge of Jesus' blood. We know only about the blood being shed -- and not about its being sprinkled!

The first biblical reference to the sprinkling of blood is in Exodus 12:22. The Israelites were commanded to take a bunch of hyssop, dip it in the blood of a slain lamb, and sprinkle it onto the lintel and two side-posts of their front door. That night, when the death angel came and saw the blood on the door posts, he would pass over the house.

Please understand—as long as the blood was left in the basin, it was of no effect; it was merely blood that had been shed. The blood had power to save only when it was lifted out of the basin and sprinkled!

Why couldn't the Israelites have simply laid the basin of blood at the threshold and said, "It doesn't matter what we do with it. After all, blood is blood"? Suppose they had put the basin on a linen-covered table, or on a pedestal just inside the door?

I'll tell you what would have happened: The death angel would have struck that home! The blood had to be lifted out of the basin and sprinkled on the door to fulfill its purpose of protection.

This blood in Exodus 12 is a type of the blood of Christ. The blood that flowed at Calvary was not wasted—it did not fall to the ground and disappear. No, that precious blood was collected in a heavenly fountain.

There is a gospel song that says, "There is a fountain filled with blood, and sinners plunged beneath that flow lose all their guilt and stain..." Yet this concept isn't scriptural; we don't plunge into the blood or swim in it. No—it is sprinkled on us!

If Christ is Lord of your life, then your door posts—your heart—have been sprinkled by His blood. And this sprinkling is not for forgiveness only—but also for protection!

When you are sprinkled,

you are totally under the protection of Christ's blood, against all the destroying powers of Satan. When his forces see Christ's blood on your door posts, they must pass over you. They cannot touch you—because they cannot touch anyone sprinkled with Christ's blood!

So, you see, the preciousness of the blood has to do with much more than forgiveness. Jesus' blood has not been left in the basin—but has been lifted out and sprinkled on your heart. And it is waiting to be sprinkled on the door posts of hearts around the world!

There is also a sprinkling of blood mentioned in Exodus 24:1-11. In this passage, God made a covenant agreement with Israel. He promised, "If you will obey My words, I will be a God to you, and you will be My people." After Moses read the law to the people, they answered, "We understand -- and we will obey." They agreed to the covenant with the Lord.

Now, this covenant had to be sealed—to be ratified and made valid—and that could happen only through the sprinkling of the blood upon it. Hebrews tells us Moses **"...took the blood...and sprinkled both the book, and all the people..."** (Hebrews 9:19).

...THE SPRINKLING OF THE BLOOD GAVE THE ISRAELITES FULL ACCESS TO GOD, WITH JOY.

The shed blood of the burnt offerings was contained in a basin. Moses took some of this blood and poured part of it by the altar. Then he took a hyssop, dipped it in the basin and sprinkled some of the blood on the twelve pillars (representing the twelve tribes of Israel). Finally, Moses dipped the hyssop into the basin and sprinkled the blood on the people. This blood covering the people, sealed the covenant!

It is clear from the passage that the sprinkling of the blood gave the Israelites full access to God, with joy. On this occasion it had nothing to do with forgiveness and remission of sin—but, rather, with communion. They were now sanctified, cleansed—fit to be in God's presence.

Then Moses, Nadab, Abihu and the seventy elders went up to the mountain to meet God. And the Lord appeared to them, coming down a sapphire-stone walk. These men saw a table spread before them—and Scripture infers that with ease, comfort and no fear of judgment, they sat in God's presence and ate and drank with Him: **"And upon the nobles of the children of Israel he laid not his hand: also they saw God, and did eat and drink"** (Exodus 24:11).

This is simply amazing! These men could eat and drink in the very presence of God—whereas shortly before, they had feared for their lives. It was because the blood had been sprinkled—and they understood the safety, the power, the security in that. They didn't fear!

Beloved, today we are in a new covenant with Jesus Christ—a covenant sealed by His own blood. And likewise today, when His precious blood is sprinkled on your soul, it is for purposes of communion as well as cleansing. It is so that you can go boldly—with ease, without fear of judgment—into God's presence for communion. You are given access to Him, with no sin condemning you. You are free to talk to God and enjoy His company!

One of the most important sprinklings of blood was done by the high priest. Once each year he went into the Holy of Holies to make atonement, which means "reconcilation." This act was meant to wipe away the people's sins, so they could be reconciled and have communion again with the heavenly Father.

THIS WAS THE MERCY SEAT WHERE GOD "SAT."

The priest would carry into the Holy of Holies a handful of incense, a censer of burning coals of fire from the altar, and a container of blood from a slain ox. Within the Holy of Holies was an ark, on top of which sat a flat, golden top with a lip around it. This was the mercy seat, where God "sat"; it was His very presence. The mercy seat had two golden cherubim on either side, with wings spread over the seat.

After cleansing himself in an elaborate ceremony, the priest went inside the Holy of holies with great reverence and fear. He dropped the incense into the fire, causing an aroma and smoke to ascend. (This represented the prayers of Christ, interceding for His people. Jesus ever sits at the right hand of the Father, interceding for the saints.)

Then the priest dipped his finger into the blood and sprinkled it seven times on the mercy seat: **"Then he shall take of the blood of the bullock, and sprinkle it with his finger upon the mercy seat eastward; and before the mercy seat shall he sprinkle of the blood with his finger seven times"** (Leviticus 16:14).

When the blood was sprinkled on God's seat, forgiveness of all sins was accomplished, and all past sins were covered. When the high priest came out, the people knew God had accepted the sacrifice, and their sins were pardoned. Israel never doubted it!

Beloved, we too have a high priest —Jesus, our Lord. And He is our High Priest not just once a year, but for all time—to the end of the world! Jesus took His own blood to the true mercy seat—into God's presence, the Holy of Holies—and presented it for the remission of all sins, of all believers, of all time. It was a final sprinkling!

Scriptures says of this act:

"Neither by the blood of goats and calves, but by his own blood he entered in once into the holy place, having obtained eternal redemption for us" (Hebrews 9:12). **"How much more shall the blood of Christ...purge your conscience from dead works to serve the living God?"** (verse 14). **"...now to appear in the presence of God for us"** (Hebrews 9:24).

Jesus took His own blood into heaven for us! And it isn't reserved there simply as a memorial. It is to be sprinkled on all who come to Him by faith!

2. How Is the Blood of Jesus Sprinkled Upon the Heart?

It is tragic that so many believers do not enjoy the power and virtue of the blood of Jesus. Scripture makes it clear—it is important for us to know how the blood has been sprinkled on our hearts. This is done in two ways:

• **The blood is sprinkled on us by the Spirit of Christ, who dwells in us.**

Jesus sprinkles His own blood on us when, by faith, we receive His finished work at Calvary. This isn't a physical sprinkling; rather, it is a legal, spiritual transaction. He sprinkles the blood on our hearts in response to our faith. And until we truly believe in the power

of His sacrifice at Calvary, the blood of Jesus cannot produce any effect upon our souls! **"Whom God hath set forth to be a propitiation [a reconciliation] through faith in his blood..."** (Romans 3:25).

Churches around the world partake of communion regularly. Yet, Paul warns us not to "drink [the cup] unworthily." This doesn't mean merely partaking of a communion service after we've failed in some way; we know that if we repent of our sin, Jesus will forgive us and cleanse us of all iniquity.

No—I believe Paul is saying we are to discern Christ's body properly. He's talking about coming to the Lord's table, drinking of the cup symbolic of His blood—and yet not believing in the power of that blood! It has to do with sitting in condemnation and fear—not believing that Christ's blood has justified and sanctified us in God's sight.

Many believers are condemned out of the wonderful experience of the Lord's table, because they do not come to the blood in faith. Paul is saying, "No wonder so many are sickly among you. You are left weak because you do not believe in the total victory of Christ's blood!"

Such Christians are saying, in essence, "I know it's wonderful to be justified through the blood of Jesus Christ. But I still have trouble believing the Lord reckons me righteous. After all, I still haven't arrived. I still struggle."

Beloved, the truest evidence of faith is rest! If you believe with all your heart, it brings your conscience and soul into rest. And when you come to the Lord's supper and partake of the cup, you can say, "I believe I am saved, forgiven, healed, because I believe in the blood. I trust in it!"

• **The blood of Jesus is sprinkled on our soul through Holy Ghost preaching.**

When you hear Christ and

His blood being exalted in Holy Ghost preaching, you can know the blood is being sprinkled!

When Philip preached the gospel to the eunuch, that man's heart was ravished by the Word. Immediately, he begged to be baptized. Philip said to him, **"...If thou believest with all thine heart, thou mayest..."** (Acts 8:37).

Likewise, every time you take to heart Holy-Ghost-anointed preaching, crying, "Lord, please, give me all Your truth"—you are being sprinkled with Christ's blood, by faith!

At this point, you may be wondering, "How can I know whether the blood has been applied to my heart?" Here are three ways you can know if you have been sprinkled by the blood:

1. If you are now willing to walk in the light and allow the Holy Ghost to expose all darkness in you, you can know you've been sprinkled.

"But if we walk in the light, as he is in the light, we have fellowship one with another, and the blood of Jesus Christ his Son cleanseth us from all sin" (1 John 1:7).

John is clearly talking about someone who is in love with the Word, unafraid of reproof—who says, "Lord, shine Your Holy-Ghost light into every crevice of my heart. I want to walk in the light." If you love the light, it's a sure sign you've been sprinkled!

2. If you call on the power and authority of Christ's blood when you're under enemy attack, you can know you've been sprinkled.

All too often, those in trouble call their best friend or a counselor, or they wallow in fear and condemnation. But those sprinkled with blood immediately stand on Jesus' blood!

We often hear the phrase

"pleading the blood" used in Christian circles. But that is not a Scriptural term. The word plead here means "argument"; it suggests begging, beseeching. And that is a defensive mode.

I believe our attitude must be stronger than that. We are warriors—blood-bought, blood-saved, more than conquerors through Jesus Christ! We are not in a courtroom with the devil, pleading a case. No—we are victors! Jesus has won the victory for us; His blood has prevailed. And I believe our battle cry should be, "I proclaim the victory of the blood of Jesus! I am blood-washed, blood-bought, blood-justified, blood-safe, blood-ransomed. And I proclaim the victory of the blood of Jesus!"

3. When you are so secure in the cleansing, justifying power of the blood that your conscience no longer condemns you, you can know you've been sprinkled.

Your conscience does an evil work when it does not wake you or stir you to obedience to the gospel. It does evil when it unnecessarily condemns you, accuses you, constantly reminds you of how you failed God, causes depression and fear.

But when you fully rest in the cleansing, justifying power of the blood of Jesus—when you take command of your conscience in the Spirit—your conscience is no longer an accuser, but, rather, does its work properly. When the devil rises up with an evil accusation, your conscience proclaims the victory of the blood!

"Let us draw near with a true heart in full assurance of faith, having our hearts sprinkled from an evil conscience..." (Hebrews 10:22). A peaceful, purged conscience is a sign of being sprinkled with His blood!

3. What Are the Benefits That Flow From the Blood of Jesus, Once Your Heart Has Been Sprinkled?

• Jesus' blood redeems us from sin and the power of darkness.

"In whom we have redemption through his blood..." (Ephesians 1:7). We are no longer under condemnation or fear!

A lot of people have been redeeemed and justified by the blood—but they don't enjoy the benefit of it, because they live in fear and condemnation. They've given faith to the Lord—but they haven't entered into the glory of being justified by the blood.

They're like a man who has built up a huge debt and can't pay it. The man's wealthy boss comes along and pays the bill without telling his employee—then calls him in to give him the good news.

The man sits down, is handed the dossier of debts, and flips through the pages to see the list of bills he has accumulated. He thinks, "I'll never be able to pay all this. They're going to throw me in jail!"

When the CEO sees the man's fearful countenance, he is perplexed. He says, "Excuse me — did you look at page one?" The man flips back to the first page, which reads: "Paid in full."

Many Christians are just like this man: They don't know their sin has been covered, paid in full! We have to enter into that knowledge by faith in order to have the benefit —which is peace with God!

• Jesus' blood has purchased the whole church of God.
"...feed the church of God, which he hath purchased with his own blood" (Acts 20:28).

Christ's church is not for sale! Forget the idea of Satan bringing down His church. Don't

wring your hands and moan, "Oh, no, the church is going to hell." No—it is going to heaven! Why? It has been blood-bought for eternity!

• Jesus' blood breaks down all walls.

"But now in Christ Jesus ye who sometimes were far off are made nigh by the blood of Christ. For he is our peace, who hath made both one, and broken down the middle wall of partition between us" (Ephesians 2:13-14).

At Times Square Church, this has great meaning. More than seventy nationalities worship here, but our church has no walls, no nationalities. We are all one in Christ—a blood-sprinkled church. Indeed, those who are blood-sprinkled no longer have any walls. They've all come down!

• Jesus' blood sanctifies us.
"...the blood of Jesus Christ his Son cleanseth us from all sin" (1 John 1:7). This ought to put a big faith-smile on your face. You are sanctified—sprinkled clean! This is a continuing work of the Spirit.

• Christ's blood overcomes Satan and puts him to flight.
"And they overcame him [the devil] by the blood of the Lamb, and by the word of their testimony..." (Revelation 12:11). What is the word of the testimony? It is simply this: "I believe in the blood! I testify to the prevailing, overcoming power of the blood of Jesus—and I proclaim its total victory!"

If you want to overcome the devil, stand on the blood—and proclaim its power!

• The blood gives us access to the Holy of Holies -- to our heavenly Father—without reproach.

"Having therefore, brethren, boldness to enter into the holiest by the blood of Jesus" (Hebrews 10:19). We are to come to our Father boldly—without fear!

4. What Does God Expect of Us Once We Are Sprinkled With the Blood of Jesus?

Are we obligated in any way by this sprinkling? Yes—very much so! If we have been sprinkled by the blood of Jesus, we are commanded to do two things:

1. We are to go in peace—and doubt no more!

When Moses sprinkled blood on the sinning Israelites, they never once doubted they were pardoned and accepted by God. They trusted in that sprinkling!

Today, the blood sprinkled on us is not that of bulls, goats or sheep—but of Christ, the Lamb of God. And yet we have more doubt, more fear than those Israelites!

Martin Luther said it is blasphemy to take back to ourselves all the sins that were laid on Christ. I agree! It is absolute sacrilege to go about in fear, guilt, condemnation—to say, "The Bible says that by faith I am cleansed, justified and protected from Satan's power—yet I can't believe such a glorious thing is possible!"

2. We are to praise God with a thankful heart—never doubting!

We are commanded to thank God for the precious blood of Jesus, with high praises:

• **"...we also joy in God through our Lord Jesus Christ, by whom we have now received the atonement"** (Romans 5:11).

• **"Be glad in the Lord, and rejoice ye righteous: and shout for joy, all ye that are upright in heart"** (Psalm 32:11).

• **"Blessed is the people that know the joyful sound..."** (89:15).

• **"I will greatly rejoice in the Lord, my soul shall be joyful in my God; for he hath clothed me with the garments of salvation, he hath covered me with the robe of righteousness..."** (Isaiah 61:10).

Proclaim the victory of Jesus' blood in your life. And begin praising Him now for the promise of that great day of redemption ahead. Amen!

—David Wilkerson died in 2011. He was the founding pastor of Times Square Church in New York City, where he ministered to gang members and drug addicts. In 1971, he founded World Challenge, Inc., which supports missionaries and outreaches throughout the world.

Reprinted by permission: World Challenge, Inc., PO Box 260, Lindale, TX 75771. http://worldchallenge.org

REACHING THE NATIONS

by Ed Silvoso

Historically Argentina has been void spiritually. Churches were very small; they were not growing at all. The believers were divided, angry at each other. But then God began to do something about 10 years ago, and the whole scene began to change.

One of the characteristics of the revival in Argentina is its passion for the lost. So many times we have a romantic idea of revival that is not entirely biblical. And when people pray for revival, they pray for the glory and the presence of God, holiness and fellowship. But if that's all you want, drop dead and go to heaven. The devil will not be around to bother you, and your flesh will not be in your way.

I believe that the purpose of revival is to make us more like Jesus. And once we become more like Him, we are to focus on those that He came to seek and to save – the lost. So the revival that doesn't have as its ultimate result the salvation of the lost by the millions is not a true revival. It's just a poor imitation of heaven.

Revelation 12:11 says, "They (believers) overcame him (Satan) by the blood of the Lamb and by the word of their testimony, and they did not love their lives to the death." We will overcome the devil. That's excellent news, isn't it?

But how do we accomplish that? By bringing together three components: First, the blood of Jesus; He already provided it once and for all. Secondly, the word of our testimony. We have emphasized that who we are in Christ gives us the victory. But it's not who you are in Christ. It's when you stand your ground and declare to the devil the truth that Christ is in you. All the time the devil is lying to us, we will not have enough money, we will not overcome a secret habit, we will not see our churches grow, we will not be able to see a breakthrough in our lives. That's why we need to tell him who we are, so that when we resist him he will flee from us.

It doesn't matter how you feel. You see, some days I wake up and I don't feel like I'm spiritual. Some days I'm in so much pain physically that I don't feel like smiling. It doesn't make any difference. It's who I am and who I say I am that the devil fears.

At Calvary, when Jesus faced the devil and all his demons, and He was momentarily forsaken by the Father, the weapon He chose was grace. Paul pled with the Corinthians "not to receive the grace of God in vain" (II Cor. 6:1). That means it is possible to receive the grace of God and not make full use of it. We cannot reach a nation unless we understand the grace of God properly and can apply it to areas of our lives where tremendous evil has taken place – whether we did it, or somebody did it to us. It's not technology, methods or programs that will reach the nations; it's the cross of Jesus and the grace flowing from it as it is incarnated in all of us.

About 1991, God allowed us to work with the pastors in an Argentinean city of 400,000 called Resistentia, where there were 5,300 believers. The city was under the power of a principality called Santo Muerto (Saint Death). Following tradition and folklore, the people made covenant with this "saint" as early as two years of age. So the whole city was demonized, the Church was in disarray, and the number of believers was insignificant.

But by the grace of God a group of seven pastors began to pray together, and things began to happen. Because the city was prayed for house by house, family by family, individual by individual, and every neighborhood was prayer walked and every home was blessed, the number of believers doubled almost immediately. The governor became a Christian, as did the mayor and five of the seven judges. The school system was flooded with conversations. In two years, the church grew 500%. The seven pastors today control the spiritual climate of the city. The authorities come to the pastor's meeting for prayer every time they have a problem that requires a miracle.

There is a biblical basis for what happened in Resistentia, and it is being used today to reach the entire nation of Argentina for Christ: "You shall receive power when the Holy Spirit has come upon you; and you shall be My witnesses both in Jerusalem, and in all Judea and Samaria, and even to the remotest part of the earth" (Acts 1:8). The power that the Lord promised is not for our personal benefit; it's for the benefit of the lost the world over. If you ask power for your problems you will get a little bit of power, just for your problems. But if you ask for power to reach the world, your problems will be taken care of, because you are mobilized for war.

—All Scripture NAS unless otherwised noted.

Ed Silvosa is the founder and president of Harvest Evangelism, Inc. A native of Argentina, he is widely recognized as a teacher on evangelism, restoration and Church unity and has extensive experience as a family counselor. He and his wife, Ruth, reside in San Jose, California.

Reprinted by permission: Christ for the Nations CFNI, P.O. Box 769000, Dallas, TX 75376-9000, 800-933-2364

LESSON 3

WALKING IN CHRIST'S AUTHORITY (UNDERSTANDING WHO WE ARE)

MAIN PRINCIPLE

Are we a victim or a victor?
Spiritual warfare does not come with an option. As soon as we accept Jesus we have joined His forces. However, when we understand the authority the Lord has given us and our identity in Christ, we will become victorious.

THE WARFARE OF PEACE

by Joyce Meyer

MOST OF US THINK SPIRITUAL WARFARE MEANS SCREAMING AT THE DEVIL AND STOMPING OUR FEET. WE DON'T REALIZE THAT RESISTING THE ENEMY INVOLVES OBEDIENCE AND QUIET RESOLVE.

During my first several years as a Christian, I listened to a lot of teaching on spiritual warfare. I tried to learn all I could about defeating the devil because it was obvious he was giving me a lot of trouble. I wanted the upper hand for a change.

Yet it seemed I gained no victory from applying all the methods I had learned –until the Lord graciously shared some truths that have become a blessing in my life.

He showed me that spiritual warfare *methods* are good, but they are only *carriers*, or containers, of His real power. I was busy rebuking, resisting, casting out and off, binding and loosing, fasting and praying, and anything else that anyone told me to do. The results were minimal, and I was worn out.

I was approaching the point of spiritual burnout. This always occurs when a Christian continues to do things that do not produce positive results.

But God opened a whole new way of looking at spiritual warfare after He challenged me to observe how Jesus dealt with the devil. As I did, I saw Christ did not do a lot of the things I had been doing.

THE WEAPONS OF LOVE AND OBEDIENCE

For example, I learned that *remaining obedient* is spiritual warfare. We often quote only a portion of James 4:7: "Resist the devil, and he will flee."

I was busy resisting, but he was not fleeing! Then I saw the whole verse: "So be subject to God. Resist the devil [stand firm against him], and he will flee from you" (Amplified).

The first part about submitting to God is equally as important as the second part about resisting the devil! I realized I was not as concerned about submitting as I was about resisting. It was a relief to find that my obedience would cause the devil to flee from me.

The Holy Spirit also revealed that *walking in love* is spiritual warfare. The devil cannot handle a lover! He could not control Jesus because He walked in obedience and love. Jesus was always loving people and being good to them.

The Word of God instructs us to keep ourselves "in the love of God" (Jude 1:21). It also tells us that in the last days "the love of the great body of people [the church] will grow cold" (Matt. 24:12).

This latter verse tells us that *cold love* will be one of the signs of the last days. Yet, Peter admonishes us: "Above all things have intense and unfailing love for one another, for love covers a multitude of sins [forgives and disregards the offenses of others]" (1 Pet. 4:8). The devil brings offense, disharmony and strife between people, but the antidote for the whole poisonous problem is love.

We can rebuke all the devils in the world-literally scream at them until we have no voice left--but they will not flee from the person who isn't walking in obedience and love.

June 1996, Charisma

Satan knows that Christians who "talk the talk" but do not "walk the walk" are powerless against him. His end-time warfare strategy is to build a stronghold of cold love. In this way he can keep the church of Jesus Christ powerless.

But by remaining in obedience, walking in love and living in a third element—peace—we can wage spiritual warfare and defeat the devil's tactics.

RESTING IN GOD'S ABILITY

Scripture tells us the believer is seated in heavenly places with Christ Jesus (Eph. 2:6). *Seated* refers to rest. Rest and peace are equivalent to each other.

The book of Hebrews teaches us to enter the rest of God and cease from the weariness and pain of human labor (see Heb. 4:3, 10-11). This rest is and has been available to us since Jesus came, died for us, was resurrected from the dead and ascended on high.

Rest is available, but we are encouraged to *enter* it. We enter the rest of God by believing His Word and by trusting in Him instead of ourselves or someone else.

We actually do spiritual warfare while we rest: "And do not [for a moment] be frightened or intimidated in anything by your opponents and adversaries, for such [constancy and fearlessness] will be a clear sign (proof and seal) to them of [their impending] destruction, but [a sure token and evidence] of your deliverance and salvation, and that from God" (Phil. 1:28).

Constancy refers to being the same--stable and consistent. It is a sign to the enemy of his impending destruction.

Our rest in peace and joy during the devil's attack literally defeats him. He cannot handle a believer who knows how to *hold his peace.*

Consistency is also an outward sign that we are trusting God. It is trust that moves Him to deliver us. We benefit when we defeat the devil, but Jesus also benefits. It gives Him glory when we operate according to His Word. He is able to bless us with our inheritance in Him.

Talking about the promises of God is encouraging, but possessing them is much better.

The Scripture says: "Blessed (happy, fortunate, to be envied) is the man whom You discipline and instruct, O Lord, and teach out of Your law, that You may give him power to keep himself calm in the days of adversity, until the [inevitable] pit of corruption is dug for the wicked" (Ps. 94:12-13).

God's plan is to work in our lives to bring us to the place when, during times of trouble, we can keep ourselves calm and at peace.

Jesus' followers wanted Him to set up an earthly kingdom and behave as an earthly king. They wanted Him to move against the enemy in the same way that they made war. But He taught them a different way to fight their battles.

He said, "But I say to you who are listening to Me: [in order to heed, make it a practice to] love your enemies, treat well (do good to, act nobly toward) those who detest you and pursue you with hatred, invoke blessings upon and pray for the happiness of those who curse you, implore God's blessing (favor) upon those who abuse you [who revile, reproach, disparage, and highhandedly misuse you]" (Luke 6:27-28).

This was a brand new way of thinking! Jesus had come to reveal a new and "living" way (Heb. 10:20)—one that would minister life instead of death.

PEACE WILL END THE WAR

Seeing peace as spiritual warfare may be a new way of thinking. It certainly was for me.

I had spent all of my life trying to fight my own battles. I thought when I learned about spiritual warfare that my struggles would be over. After all, I had located the culprit behind my problems; taking authority over him would put an end to the misery.

Instead, I ended up in a struggle with the devil that was not producing positive results, simply because I had the methods but not the power flowing through them. Peace, love and obedience are power!

My mind says fight the devil with fury--not peace. How can *peace* win a war?

But think about a natural war for a minute. What finally puts an end to it? One or both parties decide not to fight anymore. Even if only one party decides not to fight, the other one will eventually have to quit because there is no one to fight with.

My husband used to make me mad because he would not fight with me. I was upset and angry, and I wanted him to say just one thing so I could rail on and on. But when he saw that I was only looking for an argument, he would be quiet and tell me, "I am not going to fight with you."

Sometimes he would even get in the car and leave for a while, infuriating me even more. But how could I fight with someone who would not fight back?

If we meet our battles with peace and respond to the upsets in life with peace, then we will experience victory!

The methods that Jesus teaches us to use to be victorious

are usually the opposite of what makes sense in our heads. He tells us to sell what we have and give to the poor, and we will end up with more than what we started with (see Matt. 19:21); the first will be last, and the last will be first (see Matt. 19:30); to humble ourselves, and He will lift us up (see Matt. 18:4, 23:12; James 4:6).

Jesus conquered with meekness. He ruled with kindness. He humbled Himself and was placed far above all other authority. If we can accept these principles even though our minds cannot comprehend them, then surely we also can accept that peace is a form of spiritual warfare.

When the Israelites found the Red Sea facing them and the Egyptian army chasing them, they became frightened and cried to Moses. He told the people, "Fear not; stand still (firm, confident, undismayed) and see the salvation of the Lord which He will work for you today. For the Egyptians you have seen today you shall never see again. The Lord will fight for you, and you shall hold your peace and remain at rest" (Ex. 14:13-14).

Notice that Moses told them to hold their peace and remain at rest. Why? They were in warfare, and it was necessary for them to respond in peace in order to win the battle! God would fight for them if they would show their confidence in Him by being peaceful.

When trouble comes, our first temptation is to get upset, speak from our emotions, start trying first one thing and then another, and hope to find something that will work to turn the situation around. All of these are unacceptable behavior for the believer who is walking in faith. None of them will bring victory!

We are instructed to hold our peace. Jesus gave us peace. It is our inheritance. The devil regularly attempts to steal it, but it is ours, and we must hold on to it.

What God gives us is ours. But we can keep it, use it, lose it or give it away. Adam was given dominion over the earth, and he gave it to Satan, who is referred to as "the god of this world" (2 Cor. 4:4).

The Lord God did not create Satan to be the god of this world, so how did he obtain that title? Adam gave up what God had given him.

Let's not make the same mistake with those things that have been given back to us through Jesus Christ. Our inheritance is truly awesome.

Peace is a portion of it--a very important portion. Let a holy determination rise up within you to keep your peace and enjoy it.

And when you go into battle, remember to wear your "shoes of peace." God supplies us with the armor of a heavily armed soldier. He equips us for battle with righteousness, truth, peace, salvation, the Word, faith and prayer (see Eph. 6:13-18).

But many of God's children carry their armor instead of wearing it. Don't carry your shoes of peace with you like a possession; wear them!

Remember, peace is spiritual warfare. Hold your peace, live in obedience, walk in love, and you'll win the battle.

—Joyce Meyer is the founder of Life in the Word ministry in Fenton, Missouri. She is the author of several books and more than 200 stations worldwide carry her Life in the Word radio program and Life in the Word

With Joyce Meyer TV show. She often talks about the abuse she suffered as a child and her failed first marriage. She uses her personal setbacks as real life examples of the power of God in overcoming hardship.

Reprinted by permission Charisma Magazine and Strang Communications Company.

DEMONS CAN'T SWIM

by David Wilkerson

The title of this message is no joke—I'm not being facetious. I believe the Bible speaks very clearly on this subject of demons: They can't swim—because they hate water!

"When the unclean spirit is gone out of a man, he walketh through dry places, seeking rest, and findeth none" (Matthew 12:43). Unclean spirits—or demons - roam about in dry places, where there is no water. (The New American Standard translates "dry places" as "waterless places.") And the "rest" they seek is <u>possession</u>—a body to live in, a dwelling place that's dry, without water of any kind.

The Bible gives us a very clear picture of this in Mark 5. Jesus was approached by a Gadarene man who was possessed by a legion of demons (that is, about 2,000 of them). When the demons saw Jesus, a spokesdemon cried out: "What have I to do with thee, Jesus, thou Son of the most high God? I adjure thee by God, that thou torment me not" (Mark 5:7).

The demon begged Jesus to send them all into a herd of swine that was grazing on a hillside nearby. I believe those unclean spirits had every intention of driving the herd into the wilderness—a dry place, where they could wait until they found other humans to inhabit.

Jesus did permit them to possess the swine—but then, Scripture says,

"The herd ran violently down a steep place into the sea (they were about 2,000;) and were choked in the sea" (verse 13). What an incredible scene!

I have often wondered why Jesus allowed those demons to enter into the hogs. Why didn't He just send them into outer darkness, where they could never harass another human?

The fact is, Jesus never said or did anything without a powerful spiritual truth behind it. And I believe this incident has great spiritual significance for us today!

As I was studying this passage, the Holy Spirit whispered to me: "Demons can't swim!" I answered, "Lord I don't know what that means. Please show me!" And He began to open to me the significance of what Jesus allowed to happen:

I believe those hogs—suddenly possessed—were compelled by the Spirit of God to run pell-mell down the hill and plunge into the sea. Jesus is Lord over all of nature—and He commanded the swine, "Go! Take them now into the sea!" That was the end of that demonic possession—the Gadarene man was saved and delivered. Yet as the hogs ran into the water, the legion of demons went screaming in terror, out into dry places because they hate water!

THROUGHOUT THE BIBLE, FROM COVER TO COVER, WATER IS A TYPE OF THE HOLY SPIRIT.

Jesus Himself said, **"He that believeth on me, as the scripture hath said, out of his belly shall flow rivers of living water. (But this he spake of the Spirit, which they that believe on him should receive)"** John 7:38-39).

The Holy Spirit is living water! He falls like rain (both the former and latter rains). He springs up like a well within thirsting believers. And His life is poured out as a flood upon the world—like streams in the desert!

When I say demons can't stand water, I am talking about the Holy Spirit! Every demon in hell knows that water in the Bible represents God's Spirit. And they know that since Jesus is now bodily with the Father, their arch enemy is His Spirit—and wherever He abides, they must flee! They can't stand the water of the Holy Ghost—in you, in the church or in the world. And the sea that the swine were driven into was a type of the Holy Spirit! This was to serve as an object lesson to all succeeding generations.

Yet dryness represents one who is void of the Spirit of God. Dry places are a type of spiritless people—God's Spirit does not dwell in them. David said, "The rebellious dwell in a dry land" (Psalm 68:6). This is true of the believer who has neglected the Lord: he has become "dry," empty of all things of God. And dead, dry churches and Christians become the dwelling places of unclean spirits. Demons roam about them, looking for rest —because dryness opens one up to demonic harassment.

SCRIPTURE CLEARLY WARNS THAT IN THESE LAST DAYS THE EARTH WILL BE INVADED BY A MAD DEVIL!

Right now, Satan and his armies of unclean spirits are pouring out their demonic fury on mankind: "Woe to the inhabiters of the earth and of the sea! for the devil is come down unto you, having great wrath, because he knoweth that he hath but a short time" (Revelation 12:12).

Already we're seeing the evidence of this:

- **America's youth are armed to the teeth with knives, assault weapons, machine guns!** We face anarchy on our streets very soon. It's happening in Chicago and Detroit, and in nearly all major cities. Already in New York many housing developments have become war zones. A few weeks ago a young minister was shot in the head while passing out literature—cut down in the cross fire of a gang drug war!

- **Legions of demonic power have possessed leaders of our society!** For example, the chancellor of New York City's school system recently introduced a curriculum that would teach first-graders that homosexuality and lesbianism are acceptable life-styles. He claims that such teaching is needed to educate children against AIDS! I ask you: who but someone with a demon-possessed mind could present such an idea with a straight face?

The blindness and deception are incredible. Yet these same deceiving spirits have now invaded the church as well! "Now the Spirit speaketh expressly, that in the latter times some shall depart from the faith, giving heed to seducing spirits, and doctrines of devils" (1 Timothy 4:1). We are seeing Paul's warnings fulfilled:

- **Anti-Semitic doctrines are sweeping through evangelical and charismatic churches.** These teachings come straight out of the pit of hell! The devil hates Jews, because God still has a covenant with them. He hates anything having to do with the covenants of God.

How could Satan get such doctrines into our churches? It is because many have become dry —empty of God! And they are now grazing grounds for demonic powers!

- **A new "Cushite doctrine" of black supremacy is se-** ducing black evangelical churches across the nation! Many white churches are teaching doctrines of white supremacy as well. These satanic teachings are whispered into the hearts of spiritually dead shepherds—and they end up being manipulated by demons, preaching doctrines of hell!

GOD SAYS THE UNBELIEVABLE TROUBLES JUST AHEAD WILL BE BEYOND ANYTHING THE WORLD HAS EVER SEEN!

Right now America is witnessing the entire breakdown of our way of life. Yet this kind of breakdown is not just happening here—it's worldwide:

In Germany, young people are full of hate, especially toward immigrants from Eastern Europe. They are burning down housing projects where the immigrants are taken in. They especially hate Romanians, who are not even allowed to hold jobs.

Yugoslavia is being ripped apart by demonic strife, and Russia is still being torn by ethnic strife. There are wars and rumors of wars. I see terror coming to this world on all fronts: looting, killing, no respect for life or property; schools out of control, government with no solutions; earthquakes, hurricanes and tornadoes such as we have never seen.

Sometimes, as I see these things coming, I think to myself: "Lord, I'm tired of all this I—want to go home and be with You. I don't want to be here when all hell spills over!" But beloved, God has no intention of letting demons frighten His church! He is not about to stand by and let a mad devil take over. He has a glorious war plan—a sure-fire way to send unclean spirits into a chaotic frenzy:

GOD PROMISES TO ISSUE OUT OF HIS HOUSE LIVING WATERS!

God is going to send forth floods of water on dry ground, where devils work! He is going to have well-watered gardens where before there was only dryness. How? you ask. He is going to chase demons out of His house by flooding it with His Spirit! We see a picture of this in Ezekiel 47. The Lord showed Ezekiel a vision in which His Spirit overflowed and became "waters to swim in":

"He brought me again unto the door of the house; and, behold, waters issued out from under the threshold of the house" (verse 1). Ezekiel saw water begin to trickle out from under the doorway of the Lord's house. First it came up to the prophet's ankles... then to his knees... then to his loins... until finally, he said, **"It was a river that I could not pass over: for the waters were risen, waters to swim in, a river that could not be passed over"** (Ezekiel 47:5).

Then the Lord said to Ezekiel: "Every thing that liveth, which moveth, withersoever the rivers shall come shall live" (verse 9). In other words: "Wherever this river flows, there's going to be life. Living water will flow out from My house!"

Beloved, that house signifies us! We are God's house—our bodies are temples of His Holy Spirit! And the Holy Ghost is a well that continually springs up within us: **"The water that I shall give him shall be in him a well of water springing up into everlasting life"** (John 4:14).

WHEN YOU GET ALONE WITH JESUS TO WORSHIP AND ADORE HIM, THOSE LIVING WATERS BEGIN TO FLOW!

That is how God is going to fight the devil's invasion! No demon can hang around when the Holy Ghost's water is flowing within you. He'll flee to a dry place!

God sees every heart that is thirsty—and He is going to open up rivers of His Spirit for all who cry out to Him. Isaiah prophesied:

"Fear thou not; for I am with thee: be not dismayed, for I am thy God: I will strengthen thee ... they that war against thee shall be as nothing.... For I the Lord thy God will hold thy right hand.... When the poor and needy seek water, and there is none, and their tongue faileth for thirst, I the Lord will hear them... I will open rivers in high places, and fountains in the midst of the valleys: I will make the wilderness a pool of water, and the dry land springs of water" (Isaiah 41:10-18).

God is saying to us, "Don't worry about the devil taking over. I'm about to pour out My glory! All the dry places where seducing devils roam about will be turned into places of praise and glory to Me. The wilderness will become a lake of life!"

This flood of water is going to chase away all demonic powers and turn the dry places into gardens: "In the habitation of dragons, where each lay, shall be grass with reeds and rushes" (Is 35:7). According to Isaiah, it's all going to sprout and grow with life —because God will chase all dragons of death away!

Yet the promise is not just for us, but for our children as well: "I will pour my spirit upon thy seed [your children], and my blessing upon thine offspring: and they shall spring up as among the grass, as willows by the water courses" (Isaiah 44:3-4).

God has given us His everlasting word that He will fill our offspring with the very life of Jesus Christ! I am claiming this promise for the young people in our churches—the promise of a Holy Ghost flood—so that demonic powers will flee from them in terror, losing their influence and hold upon them!

Are you worried or fearful about the future? Do you wonder if a mad devil has become temporarily more powerful than our Lord? God says to you: "Is my hand shortened at all, that it cannot redeem? or have I no power to deliver? behold, at my rebuke I dry up the sea, I make the rivers a wilderness" (Isaiah 50:2).

The Lord is able to turn our school systems upside down with His Spirit! He says, "I am the One who controls the waters. I merely speak the word, and there comes either flood or drought!" Isaiah prophesied: "Say to them that are of a fearful heart, Be strong, fear not: behold, your God will come with vengeance, even God with a recompense; he will come and save you.... For in the wilderness shall waters break out, and streams in the desert. And the parched ground shall become a pool, and the thirsty lands springs of water" (Isaiah 35:4-7).

God says His waters will break out! (The New American Standard translates this phrase, "gush out.") To "break out" means to come with such force that it overflows all boundaries—flooding all surrounding areas!

Beloved, when your church becomes flooded with the water of the Spirit, the other dry churches in town will get some of the overflow. It will probably happen like this: Suddenly, in the middle of a service, someone will get a little touch of the Holy Ghost—which has overflowed from your church. He'll get out of his seat and walk toward the altar. And he'll cry out, "Pastor, I want to be saved!"

The pastor and his elders won't know what to do. But God is going to reach every thirsty heart! And whether the congregation wants it or not, the Holy Ghost is going to flood through the thirsty hearts in that dead, dry church—and mighty and wonderful things will happen!

WHAT GOD HAS PROMISED US THROUGH HIS PROPHETS IS AMAZING AND GLORIOUS!

Ezekiel prophesied that the flood is going to flow in ever-increasing intensity. It will grow from a trickle... to a river... and finally to an ocean to swim in!

Some would say, "Wonderful! We want the Holy Spirit to gush out of us. We'll just gather together to pray and believe God to open the windows of heaven and flood down upon us. We'll sit here in faith and wait for the gush to come."

No—the Bible says something altogether different! The water was only a small trickle when it was in the house; it increased in intensity only when it got to the outer gate. You see, God's water flows through us—but it cannot become a sea to swim in until it flows outside His house!

If we keep this living water to ourselves, we will enjoy a measure of life. But if we want to see demons put to confusion in all of society, the water has to pour out of us! Every true believer is to be a

fountain—overflowing outside the walls. We are to be wells that spring up and gush—not just in church, but in our home, on the job, on the street—everywhere we go!

As Ezekiel watched the flood turn into an ocean, the Lord told him to come up out of the water and look back over the banks that once were barren. "Then he brought me, and caused me to return to the brink of the river. Now when I had returned, behold, at the bank of the river were very many trees on the one side and on the other" (Ezekiel 47:6-7).

What a wonderful sight! Once there had been nothing but dryness—but now multitudes of trees had grown. In fact, everywhere the water flowed, life had sprung up. **"And it shall come to pass, that every thing that liveth, which moveth, whithersoever the rivers shall come, shall live"** (verse 9). All death had departed -- every demon had fled!

If there is a promised latter rain to come—a final, great outpouring of the Spirit—then a great harvest of souls is inevitable. Ezekiel saw this and said: "There shall be a very great multitude of fish, because these waters shall come thither" (verse 9). That means a catch of exceedingly many fish—multitudes of souls saved!

The vision was so overwhelming, Ezekiel couldn't comprehend it all. Beloved, it is because he was seeing our generation! He was prophesying that we will witness more of God's flow than any past generation ever did!

Years ago, when I saw Ezekiel's prophecy, I prayed for God to let His flood flow through me. The Lord said to me: "David, if there is nothing in you that blocks the moving of My water—if you've got the sweet fountain of Jesus in you —then everything you preach and

say in the Spirit is going to produce life!"

Dear saint, if you have His life in you, then you are spreading life because life produces life!

IN LIGHT OF ALL THESE PROPHECIES, I ASK YOU: WHAT IS COMING OUT OF YOU? LIFE—OR DEATH?

"Doth a fountain send forth at the same place sweet water and bitter?" (James 3:11).

I believe that many who read this message are going to be shocked on Judgment Day. They are going to wake up to the truth that they have neglected and departed from the Lord!

"How shall we escape, if we neglect so great a salvation?" (Hebrews 2:3). To neglect means to "be careless of" —to act as if something doesn't really matter. And this verse comes immediately after the warning "to give more earnest heed to the things which we have heard, lest at any time we should let them slip" (verse 1).

Suppose I knocked on your door today, looked you in the eye and said: "I've been sent by the Lord to warn you of something dangerous in your spiritual life. And I have a word for you, directly from God's throne: You are not going to make it! You will not be with us in glory—you're marked for eternal hell. You have opened yourself up to demonic activity, because your heart is dry and empty!"

No doubt, you would be offended. You'd say, "That can't be! I praise and worship God with my hands upraised. I feel the Spirit move on me. How could I be a dry place where demons seek rest?"

My answer would be: "What you receive in such meetings isn't from your own well. It is the overflow of living water that God pours out upon awakened saints all around you! They walk daily in the Spirit, they commune daily with Jesus—and they have developed the up-welling of the Spirit of God. But your well is bone-dry! Ever since you've known the Lord, you've had time for everything but Him. And you have done just what He has warned against: you have neglected your great salvation! You have departed from Him in your heart!"

"But," you argue, "I love people—I'll do anything for anybody. I'm not living in sin. I pray, I give. Don't tell me I don't love Jesus —you're judging me. God knows my heart!"

I would answer: "Yes, He does know your heart—and He sees every hour of your day! But you don't hunger and thirst for Him. You don't take the time to pray or dig into His word. Instead, you let it all slip by as if it really doesn't matter."

"Neglect has become a way of life for you—it has turned your heart into a dry wilderness! That is why you are so harassed, depressed and bitter at times. It is why you are attacked so often in your body. If the Spirit were flowing in you daily, all unclean spirits would have fled. But instead, you have become a dry ground—open to demonic harassment!"

Beloved, I am not suggesting that all sickness is the result of demon activity. Nor am I saying we need to pray and read the Bible all day long. God has made time for us to rest, play and enjoy our family and the good things He provides. He is not a hard taskmaster.

But when your whole day is spent on self, family, work and play, and not one hour for the Lord— not fifteen minutes to be refreshed by fellowship with Him—that is neglect! That is acting as if it does not matter! And on Judgment Day,

God will show more mercy toward the addict, the fornicator and the drunkard than He will toward you!

Soon it will be too late for you! You may think that when the world literally begins to fall apart, perhaps then you'll start to seek Him. But your heart will be so dry and empty, you'll have nothing to draw on. You won't want to pray. Instead, your condition will get worse—and you'll grow harder and colder than ever. When you come to church and see others running to God because they know the hour of judgment has come, you'll be so harassed and confused you won't know what to do! If you won't come while His mercy is available you won't come during the flood of judgments!

IF ALL OF GOD'S PEOPLE CAME TO HIS HOUSE FULL OF THE WATER OF THE SPIRIT, WE WOULD NEVER HAVE TO BIND DEMON POWERS OR REBELLIOUS SPIRITS!

There would be such an ocean of God's Spirit, all demonic powers would flee in panic. There would be a breaking forth of His glory like nothing we have ever seen. No sinner could remain neutral!

But what breaks God's heart most of all is that the majority of those who neglect Him are the ones He so wants to use as soul-winners. You could have your fountain opened up—the Spirit could flow His life-giving water through you. You could be a life-giver instead of a dry bush in the desert. Is God's life-bringing water springing up out of you daily? Or have you become a dead, dry well? God has so much in store for you, if you

will only repent and confess your neglect to Him. Call out to Him now:

"Lord—I have been dry for so long. I have neglected You and departed from You in spirit. Forgive me! I'm so dry, so lifeless. Fill me with Your life-giving water—drive all harassing spirits away.

"Flood my soul, Lord! I want to experience Your life-giving flow. Use me—and let me see Your ocean of living water poured out in my life!"

Amen!

—David Wilkerson died in 2011. He was the founding pastor of Times Square Church in New York City, where he ministered to gang members and drug addicts. In 1971, he founded World Challenge, Inc., which supports missionaries and outreaches throughout the world.

Reprinted by permission: World Challenge, Inc., PO Box 260, Lindale, TX 75771. http://worldchallenge.org

LESSON 4

KNOWING OUR ENEMY

MAIN PRINCIPLE

Just to recognize the enemy is not enough. We also need to know what he is capable of and where he stands in comparison to God.

HOW TO SILENCE SATAN

by Terry Law

Have you ever wondered how to silence the accusations of Satan, how to take authority over his constant barrage against the will of God in your life? There is a way for us to silence him, but first we have to understand how he works against us.

Revelations 16:13-14 gives us a graphic illustration of how Satan attacks. *And I saw coming out of the mouth of the dragon and out of the mouth of the beast and out of the mouth of the false prophet, three unclean spirits like frogs; for they are spirits of demons, performing signs, which go out to the kings of the whole world, to gather them together for the war of the great day of God, the Almighty.* Notice the repetition of the phrase, "out of the mouth." It will provide a key principle later on.

Now look at Psalm 8:1-2. *O Lord, our Lord, how majestic is Thy name in all the earth, who hast displayed Thy splendor above the heavens! From the mouth of infants and nursing babes Thou hast established strength, because of Thine adversaries, to make the enemy and the revengeful cease.* This verse makes one thing clear: the enemy needs to be silenced; therefore, he must be making a lot of noise.

Looking back to Revelation 16, we see an illustration of unclean spirits which the Bible likens to frogs.

Have you ever listened to frogs? Out of all God's creatures, they are probably the most boring, repetitious creatures. They make the same sound, in the same way, for hours on end, never changing their rhythm or pitch.

Having spent so much time in the Soviet Union, I have made an association between frogs and the propaganda the Soviet government constantly puts out. It has no melody to it and makes no sense...it is a constant droning of doctrine.

This is the same way Satan attacks God's children. He bombards them with constant propaganda which can take several different forms. "You're a failure...God doesn't love you...If you were really a Christian, you wouldn't be sick or have financial problems, etc."

Demonic spirits have the power to convince, to bring the kings of the earth to battle. Most evil spirits operate as thoughts; fear, heaviness or depression, lying and suicide are all examples. Satan's forces are constantly croaking and trying to pull you down in your walk with Christ. If they can cause you to doubt what God has said, then they have planted unbelief in your life, and unbelief is the root of all sin.

Satan is the master of suggestions, but he does not have the power to control your thoughts. His ultimate purpose is to capture our hearts, and even more, our mouths. Once a person begins to listen to Satan's suggestions, he begins to receive and believe them and then they come out of his mouth, providing a tool Satan can use to destroy. Once Satan has your mouth, he has you and uses you for his kingdom. Still, his ability is limited to what he can get you to say. If he can get you speaking with unbelief and negativism, then you are spewing forth the sound of frogs.

Now that you see how Satan attacks us, see what you can do to stop him.

Isaiah 55:11 says this: *So shall My word be which goes forth from my mouth; it shall not return to Me empty, without accomplishing what I desire, and without succeeding in the matter for which I sent it.* God's Word contains the creative power of the universe. If your mouth is employed in the service of God, you can destroy Satan's kingdom. Therefore, a battle rages for your mouth.

Revelation 16:13-14 uses the phrase, "out of the mouth" three times. Matthew 12:37 tells us we are justified and or condemned by the words of our mouth. Proverbs 10:11 says that the mouth of a righteous man is a well of life. Proverbs 12:14 says: *A man will be satisfied with good by the fruit of his words*...These scriptures all tell us how to silence Satan – by the word of our mouth.

Psalm 149:6-9 tells us to let the high praises of God be in our mouth and a two-edged sword in our hand, to execute on the enemy the written judgment. This is the honor of all the saints. When we praise God, we minister to the enemy God's revealed judgment. When we pass sentence, the walls must come down. When we praise, the angels of the Lord do battle on our behalf, knowing that the battle has already been won!

Begin to praise the Lord with your mouth at all times. You will be amazed at the power it brings to your daily walk with Christ.

— Terry Law led his first missionary trip behind the Iron Curtain in 1968. Since then, his ministry of evangelism and worship has taken him throughout the former Soviet Union and to more than 40 countries with his Living Sound music teams. He is the president and founder of World Compassion/ Terry Law Ministries and Living Sound International in Tulsa, Oklahoma.

Reprinted with permission: Psalmist Magazine

WALKING IN THE GLORY!

By David Wilkerson

I believe there is only one thing that can keep us going in the coming hard times and that is an understanding of God's glory. Now, this may sound like a high, lofty concept to you, one that's best left to theologians. But I'm convinced the subject of God's glory has very real, practical value for every true believer. By grasping it, we unlock the door to an overcoming life!

I've already discovered two important truths in my study of this subject:

1. The glory of God is a revelation of our Lord's nature and being.

You may recall from the Old Testament that Moses got a literal glimpse of God's glory. Before then, the Lord had sent out Moses with no explanation of himself other than the words, "I AM." But Moses wanted to know something more of God. So he pleaded with him, "Lord, show me your glory."

God responded by taking Moses aside and putting him in the cleft of a rock. Then, scripture says, he revealed himself to Moses in all his glory: "The Lord passed by before him, and proclaimed, The Lord, the Lord God, merciful and gracious, longsuffering, and abundant in goodness and truth, keeping mercy for thousands, forgiving iniquity and transgression and sin "

(Exodus 34:6-7).

I believe this passage is absolutely essential to our understanding of who our Lord is. Often when we think about the glory of God, we think of his majesty and splendor, his power and dominion, or some manifestation in his people, such as boisterous worship. All such things can be a result of seeing God's glory. But this isn't the glory he wants us to know him by.

The way God wants us to know his glory is through the revelation of his great love toward humankind. And that's just what he revealed to Moses: "...the Lord God, merciful and gracious, longsuffering, and abundant in goodness and truth, keeping mercy for thousands, forgiving iniquity and transgression and sin " (Exodus 34:6-7).

The Lord is forever waiting to show us his love—to forgive us, shower us with his mercy and restore us to himself!

2. The revelation of God's glory has powerful effects on those who receive it and pray for an understanding of it.

Up to this point, Moses had viewed the Lord as a God of law and wrath. He trembled with terror in the Lord's presence—petitioning him, crying out to him, pleading with him on behalf of Israel. This had been the basis of his face-to-face relationship with the Lord.

Yet now, at the first sight of God's glory, Moses was no longer fearful of the Lord. Instead, he was moved to worship: "Moses made haste, and bowed his head toward the earth, and worshipped" (verse 8). He saw that God wasn't just the thunder, lightning and piercing trumpet that had made him shrivel in fear. On the contrary, God was love—and his nature was one of kindness and tender mercy!

Do you see the incredible truth scripture is showing us here? True worship arises from hearts that are overcome by a vision of God's unmerited love for us. It's based on the revelation that God gives us of himself—of his goodness, his mercy, his readiness to forgive. So, if we're to praise God both in spirit and in truth, our worship must be based on this awesome truth about him.

Indeed, once we receive a revelation of God's glory, our worship can't help but change. Why? Seeing his glory changes the way we live! It affects our countenance and behavior—changing us from "glory to glory," making us more like him. Each new revelation of his love and mercy brings supernatural change.

I'm convinced this is the only way lasting change occurs. It comes not from attending how-to seminars, or hearing famous speakers, or absorbing self-improvement messages from books or tapes. No —it comes from having a revelation of God, period! And God has already given us that revelation of himself, in Exodus 34.

Seeing God's glory also changes our relationships with others. Paul tells the Ephesian church, "You've seen and tasted the glory of God. Now, be a reflection of that glory to others!" "Be ye kind to one another, tenderhearted, forgiving one another, even as God for Christ's sake hath forgiven you" (Ephesians 4:32).

Now let me speak to you about walking in the glory of God.

1. THE REVELATION OF GOD'S GLORY TO US HAS EVERYTHING TO DO WITH OUR COMMUNION WITH HIM.

Many Christians talk about intimacy with the Lord—walking with him, knowing him, having fellowship with him. But we can't have true communion with God unless we receive into our hearts the full revelation of his love, grace and mercy.

Communion with God consists of two things: 1. Receiving the love of the father, and 2. loving him in return. You can spend hours each day in prayer, telling the Lord how much you love him—but that isn't communion. If you haven't received his love, you haven't had communion with him. You simply can't share intimacy with the Lord unless you're secure in his love for you.

The psalmist encourages us to "enter into (God's) gates with thanksgiving, and into his courts with praise" (Psalm 100:4). What's the reason for such praise

and thanksgiving? And why are we given such a bold invitation? It's because we're shown the kind of God we're to come to: "For the Lord is good; his mercy is everlasting; and his truth endureth to all generations" (verse 5).

I know when I come to my Lord, I'm not coming to a hard, fierce, demanding father. He doesn't wait for me with an angry countenance, anxious to put a rod to my back. He doesn't trail me, waiting for me to fail so he can say, "I caught you!"

No—I'm coming to a father who has revealed himself to me as pure, unconditional love. He's kind and tenderhearted, full of grace and mercy, anxious to lift all my cares and burdens. And I know he'll never turn me down when I call on him.

That's why I'm to come into his courts with praise and thanksgiving—because I'm thankful for who my God is. He cares about everything concerning me!

Few believers, however, have laid hold of God's love for them by faith. They live in fear and despair, with little or no hope, always facing a storm. They can't understand why their lives aren't fulfilled, why they're full of such turmoil and confusion. They often think, "I pray daily, and I read my Bible. I constantly show God how much I love him. So why don't I have rest and peace?"

It's because they've never grasped the truth that God loves them! They haven't comprehended that, in spite of all their weaknesses and failures, their heavenly father cares about everything they're going through!

TRUE LOVE IS MANIFESTED IN TWO THINGS: REST AND REJOICING.

The prophet Zephaniah says something incredible about God's love for us. He writes, "The Lord thy God in the midst of thee is mighty; he will save, he will rejoice over thee with joy; he will rest in his love, he will joy over thee with singing" (Zephaniah 3:17).

This verse tells us two important things about how the Lord loves us:

1. God rests in his love for his people.

In Hebrew, the phrase "he will rest in his love" reads, "He shall be silent because of his love." God is saying, in essence, "I've found my true love, and I'm totally satisfied! I don't need to look elsewhere, because I have no complaint. I'm completely fulfilled in this relationship, and I won't take my love back. My love is a settled matter!"

Zephaniah is telling us, "This is God's love for you! He wants you to know, I've found what I'm looking for and it's you! You bring great joy to me! "

2. God gets great pleasure from his people.

Zephaniah testifies, "He rejoices over you with singing" (see same verse). He's saying, in other words, "God's love for you is so great, it puts a song on his lips!"

To "rejoice" means to have joy and delight. It's an outward expression of internal delight. It's also the highest expression of love. The Hebrew word Zephaniah uses for "rejoice" here is "tripudiare" meaning, "to leap, as one overcome with joyful ecstasy."

Can you conceive of your heavenly father being so in love with you that he leaps with joy at the very thought of you? Can you receive his word that he loved you before the world was created, before humankind existed, before you were even born? Can you accept that he loved you even after you fell into Adam's sinful ways and became an enemy to him?

That's right—God foresaw all your sins and failures, yet he still loved you with the same tender love. In fact, he sent his Spirit to awaken you to your lost condition and your need for him. He drew you to himself, enfolding you in his arms. Then, when you came to the cross in repentance, you entered into his gift of love to you. He promised you, "I loved you then, I love you now, and I'll love you to the end!"

If God so loved you when you were deep in sin—caring enough to give his own son to die for you—why would he remove his love whenever you stumble or fail? In such times, we're to remember who he says he is to us—love, mercy, longsuffering. That is his glory —and we're to return to his glory always!

WHY DON'T MORE CHRISTIANS COMMUNE WITH THE LORD AND HAVE INTIMACY WITH HIM?

Multitudes of God's offspring know little or nothing of a life of communion with him. Why is this so?

I believe such Christians have a sad, twisted concept of the heavenly father. I recall Jesus' parable about the servant who hid his talent because he had a twisted image of his master. That servant said, "... I knew thee that thou art an hard man ..." (Matthew 25:24).

Likewise, many believers today think, "There's no way God could ever dance over me, rejoicing and singing in love. I've failed him so miserably at times, bringing reproach on his name. How could he possibly love me—especially in the struggle I'm facing now?"

I've known families in which the children cowered in the presence of a hard, mean father. They played happily before their dad came home. But when they saw him come through the door, they ran straight to their mother and clutched her apron. I never saw them go near their father, except when he demanded something of them. They never crawled into his lap or ask to be hugged. They dreaded being in his presence.

I believe this is one powerful reason why so many Christians don't want to get close to their heavenly father. They dread drawing near to him because they sense they've failed him somehow. They have a nagging feeling they've neglected their duties, been lazy spiritually, done things wrong. All they can conceive of him is that he's full of consuming fire, ready to judge and condemn them.

Such Christians think, "God has forgiven me so many times before, I can't go to him now. He'll reject me. I've got to be past the point of being forgiven." No! God never rejects anyone who turns to him in repentance. That's not his nature! We can't judge our heavenly father by the measure of our human fathers. That's not who he is.

The question for all of us today is, how can we not want to be near a father who writes love letters to us...who tells us he yearns to be with us...who's always ready to embrace us...who says he has nothing but good thoughts about us, in spite of our foolishness...who assures us, "Satan may tell you you're useless. But I say you're my joy!"

It's our unwillingness to believe his word to accept and lay hold of the marvelous revelation of his glory that keeps us from communing with him!

IT'S NOT POSSIBLE TO HAVE COMMUNION OR INTIMACY WITH THE LORD UNTIL WE BELIEVE AND RECEIVE HIM AS BEING FULL OF LOVE, TENDERNESS AND KINDNESS TOWARD US!

At this point, you may be thinking, "Surely the Lord doesn't rejoice over someone who's still in sin. I can't expect him to love me if I continue my sinning ways. That sort of thinking borders on blasphemy."

Yes, God does love his people—but he doesn't love their sin. The Bible says he reproves every child who continues in iniquity, but he always does it with longsuffering. And after he reproves us, his Spirit fills us with a sense of his indignation over our sin.

Through all of this, God's love for us remains unchanged. His word says, "I am the Lord, I change not..." (Malachi 3:6). "...the Father... with whom is no variableness, neither shadow of turning" (James 1:17). "...I am God, and not man..." (Hosea 11:9).

God forbid that his love for us should ebb and flow as ours does for him. Our love varies almost daily, going from hot and zealous to lukewarm or even cold. Like the disciples, we can be ready to die for Jesus one day and then forsake him and run the next. We can tell the Lord we trust him to supply all our needs and keep us from falling —but that isn't true communion. The question is, do we fully trust his love to us? Have we seen his love revealed and laid hold of it? Is his love for us settled in our hearts?

I must ask you—are you able to say, "My heavenly father is in love with me! He says I'm sweet and lovely in his eyes—and I believe him. I know no matter what I go through, or how tempted or tried I become, he'll rescue me. He'll hover over me through it all, never allowing me to be crushed. He'll always be kind and tender to me!"

This is when true communion begins. We're to be convinced each day of God's unchanging love for us. And we're to show him we believe his revelation about himself. John writes, "We have known and believed the love that God hath to us. God is love; and he that dwelleth in love dwelleth in God, and God in him" (1 John 4:16).

This belief alone can heal your soul. It's your only weapon against the devil, who lies that you're too unworthy to pray or draw near to God. Convincing yourself of this truth is the only way to open yourself to true communion!

If you've ever been in love with someone, you know what I'm talking about. Imagine a husband who's away on business much of the time, but who's utterly in love with his wife. He calls his beloved spouse every night he's away. And from time to time he calls home just to leave a message for her on their answering machine. His message to her goes something like this:

"Hi, honey. I m calling to let you know that just the thought you're there, loving me, brings me strength. It's going to be the lift I need for the day. I know I'm going to have a tough time with work today. But I've just read the letter you wrote to me, and oh, what a joy! Just knowing you're thinking of me makes me overflow with ecstasy!"

That's the love the heavenly father has for you. Trust in it!

THE OTHER SIDE OF COMMUNION IS OUR LOVING GOD BACK!

Walking in God's glory means not only that we receive the father's love, but that we love him back as well. It's about mutual affection—both giving and receiving love. The Bible tells us, "...thou shalt love the Lord thy God with all thine heart, and with all thy soul, and with all thy might" (Deuteronomy 6:5).

God says to us, "My son, give me thine heart " (Proverbs 23:26). His love demands that we reciprocate—that we return to him a love that's total, undivided, requiring all our heart, soul, mind and strength.

However, the Lord tells us in no uncertain terms, "You can't earn my love. The love I give to you is unmerited!" John writes, "Herein is love, not that we loved God, but that he loved us, and sent his Son to be the propitiation for our sins" (1 John 4:10). "We love him, because he first loved us" (verse 19).

We didn't wake up one day, decide to walk away from our sins, and turn to Jesus. No—the Spirit of God reached down into the wilderness of our lives, showed us our lostness and made us miserable in our sin. He sent us his word to show us truth, sent his Spirit to convict us, and then came after us himself. He did it all for us.

And now, just as God's love for us is marked by rest and rejoicing, so our love for him must have these same two elements:

1. David expresses a rest in his love for God when he writes, "Whom have I in heaven but thee? And there is none upon earth that I desire beside thee" (Psalm 73:25). The heart that loves the Lord ceases completely from looking elsewhere for comfort. Rather, it finds full contentment in him. To such a lover, God's lovingkindness is better than life itself!

2. Such a heart also rejoices in its love for God. It sings and dances in joyous ecstasy over the Lord. When a child of God knows how much his father loves him, it puts a delight in his soul!

The Bible also tells us that our love for the father must be conveyed through his son. Jesus says, "...no man cometh unto the Father, but by me" (John 14:6). It's by Christ alone that we're accepted by the father and have access to him.

Moreover, God placed all his goodness, love, mercy and grace—that is, his glory—in his son. And he sent Jesus to manifest and reveal that glory to us. Thus, Christ comes to us as the express image of our loving father. "As the Father hath loved me, so have I loved you: continue ye in my love" (John 15:9).

God loves us as we stand in Christ. And, in turn, we show love for God in our love for Jesus. As the head of the church, and as our high priest, Jesus carries our love to the father for us.

Now let me give you one of the most powerful verses in all of scripture. Proverbs give us these prophetic words of Christ: "Then I was by him, as one brought up with him: and I was daily his delight, rejoicing always before him; rejoicing in the habitable part of his earth; and my delights were with the sons of men" (Proverbs 8:30-31).

Beloved, we're the sons being mentioned here! From the very foundations of the earth, God foresaw a body of believers joined to his son. And even then the father delighted and rejoiced in these sons. Jesus testifies, "I was my father's delight, the joy of his being. And now all who turn to me in faith are his delight as well!"

So, how do we love Jesus in return? John answers, "This is the love of God, that we keep his commandments: and his commandments are not grievous" (1 John 5:3).

And what are his commandments? Jesus says, in essence, there are two—and "on these two commandments hang all the law and the prophets" (Matthew 22:40). The first and most important commandment is to love the Lord with all our heart, soul and mind. We're to hold nothing back from him. And the second is that we love our neighbor as ourselves. These two simple, non-grievous commands sum up all of God's law.

Jesus is saying here that we cannot be in communion with God —we can't walk in his glory—if we bear a grudge against anyone. Therefore, loving God means loving every brother and sister in the same way we've been loved by the father.

"If a man say, I love God, and hateth his brother, he is a liar: for he that loveth not his brother whom he hath seen, how can he love God whom he hath not seen? And this commandment have we from him, That he who loveth God love his brother also" (1 John 4:20-21). "He that loveth not knoweth not God; for God is love" (verse 8).

All communion and intimacy with the Lord is cut off if we have an unloving or unforgiving attitude toward another person. We can praise God with upraised arms, pray to him every day, spend hours studying his word—but if we're bitter and unforgiving toward anyone, it's all in vain. John says, "Such a person is a liar. You don't truly love God, even though he loves you!"

If you're in such a state, don't just say to God, "Lord, I'm sorry, forgive me." Rather, go to that person as God's word instructs, and be reconciled with him. "...first be reconciled to thy brother, and then come and offer thy gift" (Matthew 5:24).

Only then will you find true intimacy with the father. And you'll be able to walk in his glory, all the days of your life!

—David Wilkerson died in 2011. He was the founding pastor of Times Square Church in New York City, where he ministered to gang members and drug addicts. In 1971, he founded World Challenge, Inc., which supports missionaries and outreaches throughout the world.

Reprinted by permission: World Challenge, Inc., PO Box 260, Lindale, TX 75771. http://worldchallenge.org.

LESSON 5

IF THE CLOTHES FIT WEAR THEM!

MAIN PRINCIPLE

God has equipped us with spiritual armor. With the full armor of God, we are fully prepared to stand against the enemy.

EXERCISE YOUR AUTHORITY

by Marilyn Hickey

JESUS HAS GIVEN US AUTHORITY OVER THE DEVIL, BUT TOO OFTEN WE ARE NOT SURE HOW TO EXERCISE THAT AUTHORITY SO WE DO NOTHING.

What would you think of police officers who do not respond to the shriek of burglar alarms, the panicked cries of children or the sounds of automatic pistols? You would probably say they are not doing their job. But that is exactly what many Christians are doing today. Jesus has given us authority over the devil, but too often we are not sure how to exercise that authority so we do nothing. It's time we wake up and get to work.

We have an assignment, as the body of Christ on earth, to do the work of Jesus. The Bible says He was made manifest to destroy the works of the evil one (see 1 John 3:8). Because we are His body, that is our job too. We have a search-and-destroy mission: to search out the areas of the devil's attack and destroy his strongholds. This month I am presenting the first in a two-part series on "Devils, Demons and Deliverance." I want to help you focus on the areas of Satan's strongholds so we can bring down spiritual forces.

We've been equipped with the necessary tools: the Word of God, prayer, the mighty name of Jesus Christ and the power of His blood. Now let's put them into action as we bring Satan's operations to a halt.

I believe there are seven major areas of demonic power in the world today: religion, business, politics, crime, occultism, disease and morals.

It may surprise you that the first stronghold listed is religion--false demonic religion. We easily recognize the grip of the enemy over a temple full of idols in India, but what happens when we find demonic religion operating in Hometown, U.S.A.?

The Bible warns that in the latter days some will depart from the faith, succumbing to seducing spirits and doctrines of devils. From the time Satan persuaded Eve to disobey God, seducing spirits have offered the devil's lies cloaked in religious garb. That's why we need to be on guard against Satan's schemes to change our thinking by subtly adding to or subtracting from the truth. If he can get us to disobey God, we're no longer a threat to him.

How do we prevent that? We must have a standard by which everything is judged: the Word of God. Whatever doesn't stand up to the Word must be rejected as false. There are four steps we can take to guard against departing from the truth:

1. *Be familiar with your weapons.* Soldiers must learn to take their rifles apart and reassemble them so well that they can do it with their eyes closed. Do we know the Word of God that well? It's imperative we spend time reading, meditating and memorizing Scripture.

2. *Spend time with God.* As we tune our spiritual ears to hear Him, we will learn to know His voice. As we fellowship with God, we become like Him.

3. *Stop being self-centered.* If you have a need, pray for someone else with a similar need. Jesus has said if you will lose your life for His sake, you will gain it. He knows that when we focus on our own prob-

October 1993, Charisma

lems, we become critical of others. We must take our own needs to the Lord in prayer and leave them. That frees us to serve God by ministering to others.

4. *Wage spiritual warfare when you see someone in spiritual bondage.* When we recognize the hand of the devil in a person's life or situation, it is our call to spiritual warfare. We can take authority over the enemy in Jesus' name and speak the truth of God's Word into that situation.

The second stronghold is in business where greed is the basis of most business decisions. Money is the focus, and actions are judged by their dollar value. While money itself is not evil, its proper use is to glorify God. As faithful stewards, we should use our money wisely to provide for our families and to win souls for the kingdom.

How do we wage warfare in the business world? When we see greed we need to rebuke the spirits that provoke it. Stand against covetousness, deceit and other sources that you believe cause greed. Plead the blood of Jesus in the particular situation and speak the truth of God's Word over it.

The third area of demonic bondage is politics. The devil has set up principalities and powers which allow spiritual wickedness to operate in world governments. When we see ungodliness in the political system, we are to love the people involved but rebuke Satan in Jesus' name. We are to plead the blood of Jesus over nations and speak the truth of God's Word. Don't just watch or read the news— pray to change the news!

Earlier I listed crime, occultism, disease and morals as other strongholds established by Satan. The church needs to stand against the work of the evil one wherever it operates. The primary principle is to be led by the Spirit who alone comprehends the extent of the battle, the proper strategy and tactics.

Next month we will examine a controversial subject: Can a Christian be demon possessed? Also, what response is appropriate when we believe someone is under demonic oppression or control?

— Marilyn Hickey is an American minister and Christian television personality who teaches Bible studies both nationally and internationally. She and her husband Wallace, now deceased, founded the Orchard Road Christian Center, a large church in Denver, Colorado.

Reprinted by permission Charisma Magazine and Strang Communications Company.

NOT BY THE SWORD OF MAN!

by David Wilkerson

YOU CAN ENJOY TOTAL VICTORY OVER THE POWER OF SIN.

God's New Covenant with us can be summed up in one powerful statement: It is his irrevocable promise to deliver his people from the dominion of sin—through the power of the Holy Ghost!

This New Covenant does away with all of our puny efforts to please God through our flesh. It is the end of all our striving to overcome sin, whether through determination, strength, reasoning or any other works of the flesh. In short, God's New Covenant takes the pressure off of us—and places it all on him!

Through this covenant, the Lord says, "I will no longer ask you to bring me a godly heart. Instead, I will remove your heart of stone—and I'll put in you a new heart, one that has a desire for me. I will cause you both to will and to do my good pleasure, through the power of my Spirit!"

In simple terms, the New Covenant is the end of the "can do" man. This is the man in us who says, "I can do it all, in my own power and strength. If I can just spend enough time in prayer and Bible study—if I can just think through my problems

—I'll be able to make changes in my life."

God's New Covenant says goodbye to this old, "can do" man—and it introduces the "new man," who says, "I can't do anything in my own strength. I don't have the power to effect any kind of godly change in my life. But I can do everything through the power of the Holy Spirit!"

One of the most important things I've learned from my study of the New Covenant is that it is the secret to having an overcoming life in the last days. As the time of Christ's return draws near, the devil is going to open up the floodgates of hell against God's people. He will let loose wild, demonic powers such as the world has never seen.

We see this happening already within the walls of the church. Satan has infiltrated God's house with subtle lies, false doctrines, demonic teachings—and undiscerning Christians are swallowing it all. At this moment, multitudes of deceptions and heresies are swirling through the church. I ask you— how will believers be able to stand in such times?

The Lord answers us by

promising to take on the problem himself. He assures us, "Don't be afraid. I'm going to take this matter into my own hands. I will empower you against every onslaught of the enemy. And I will do it through my New Covenant with you!"

As soon as I began studying the New Covenant, I saw its glorious truths leaping out of God's Old Testament dealings with Israel. Paul states, **"All these things happened unto them for ensamples: and they are written for our admonition, upon whom the ends of the world have come"** (1 Corinthians 10:11). I sensed the Lord asking me, "David, do you want the keys to victory? Do you want to know how to overcome sin, flesh and the devil? Do you want to know how to do battle with the enemy? Then go to my Old Testament, and you will learn from the examples there. I have recorded them all for you, so you can learn the lessons of godliness!"

THE FIRST LESSON WE DRAW FROM THE OLD TESTAMENT IS JUST HOW SAFE A CHILD OF GOD IS WHEN

HE TRUSTS IN THE BLOOD!

On the night of Passover, not a single Israelite was in danger from the death angel who swept through Egypt. Every man, woman and child of God rested safely and securely under the blood covering that was spread on the doorposts of their homes. This picture of safety in the Old Testament represents the protective power of our Lord's blood over his children today. As Christians, we are to be a believing, trusting people who have the blood of Christ sprinkled on the doorposts of our hearts.

Israel's trust in the blood of the slain lamb accomplished many things in their lives. It not only protected them from the death angel, but it also brought them out of Egypt and delivered them from the bondage of Pharaoh. Yet, there were other enemies from which Israel needed deliverance. And, likewise today, our trust in the blood of Christ is about much more than obtaining salvation for eternity. It also involves relying on God's power to deliver us from every stronghold of the enemy.

Please don't mistake me here. If you are saved—living under the covering of Christ's blood, secured by faith in his work on the cross for you—that is absolutely wonderful. But what about your ongoing battle with the power of sin, which rages inside you? What about your besetting habit? What about the roaring lion who seeks to devour you? What power do you have to do battle with these enemies of your soul?

The fact is, even if we have been saved and secured by Christ's blood, we are still engaged in a battle with overwhelming principalities, satanic powers, demonic strongholds. And we are to claim the power that is available to us through God's New Covenant. But that power comes only by faith!

ISAIAH DELIVERED A STRONG MESSAGE TO THE BLOOD-SECURED CHILDREN OF ISRAEL.

The prophet Isaiah warned Israel that there was no possibility of victory for them if they attempted to fight their adversary in their own strength. Isaiah 31 paints a perfect picture of the futility of trying to do battle with the enemy in our human ability. I believe this chapter is a type and shadow of the ineffectiveness of our attempts today to defeat lusts, habits and besetting sins by relying on human ideas and aids.

At the time Isaiah wrote this message of warning, King Sennacherib and the Assyrian army had already marched through Judah. They had captured most of the cities in their path, and now they planned to besiege Jerusalem. In Hebrew, the word "Sennacherib" means "successful." And "Assyria" means "sin on the increase." Put together, these two words provide an image of an evil enemy who was having great success against God's people. Indeed, Assyria represents every sinful, demonic, lustful spirit that comes against us. And Sennacherib is the devil himself, convinced he will succeed in defeating us and bringing us into despair. I believe God wants to show us through this chapter how the devil and his demonic hordes are bringing waves of temptations against the church—with increasing intensity and much success!

This chapter is also an example to us of how sin will increase in the last days. Scripture says society will wax worse and worse, and the church will be inundated with deceptions and doctrines of demons. I believe we're seeing that happen right now. Demonic hordes have infiltrated all media and every form of technology, flooding our culture with sensuality, nudity, perversions of all kinds. As prophesied in Revelation 12, Satan has **"...cast out of his mouth water as a flood after the woman..."** (Revelation 12:15).

Hezekiah was king in Israel at the time Sennacherib and the Assyrians approached. And as he looked down on the huge army surrounding the city, his old "can do" man kicked in. The king reasoned that with just a little time, thought and some outside help, the Israelites could deliver themselves from this awful circumstance. He said, "We're facing an overwhelming situation here. Assryia is a powerful enemy. But I think all we need is a little military aid. We can probably hold off their army while we scout around for someone to help us."

So Hezekiah sent an envoy of ambassadors to Egypt, bearing gifts of silver and gold, in an attempt to hire their army for support. He thought that with the Egyptians' horses, chariots and infantry, Israel could push the Assyrians back.

Now, you may think Israel simply lacked faith in the midst of this situation. But God called their actions outright rebellion! Isaiah writes: **"Woe to them that go down to Egypt for help; and stay on horses, and trust in chariots, because they are many; and in horsemen, because they are very strong; but they look not unto the Holy One of Israel, neither seek the Lord!"** (Isaiah 31:1). God was saying, "You have revolted against me! You know I am your only source for victory. Yet you have refused to turn to me!" Israel here represents the believer who puts his trust in the flesh. Isaiah writes: **"Now the Egyptians are men, and not God; and their horses flesh, and not spirit...."** (verse 3). The prophet is saying, in essence, "You think you are able to deliver yourselves from this enemy by your own power. You think victory lies in your own strength, intellect and abilities. Yet you are trusting in mere flesh! Return now to the Lord. He is your only hope of deliverance!"

THE CHURCH TODAY HAS ITS OWN VERSIONS OF EGYPTIAN CHARIOTS!

Like Israel, many Christians today quickly turn to manmade things in an attempt to achieve victory over the flesh. One glaring example is the vast number of self-help books found on the shelves of Christian bookstores. Literally thousands of books promise surefire ways of improving our flesh, appeasing our flesh, subduing our flesh. Indeed, everywhere we turn, we're offered fleshly options to all our needs. Churches promise anointed revival meetings where we can have all our spiritual needs fulfilled by a prayer or a touch. Evangelists offer instant deliverance, instant healing, instant words from God.

The truth is, God gave Israel the option of choosing himself or the flesh in the midst of their situation. He said, "Go ahead and exercise your own will. Dig deeply into your inner man, and pull out all of your strengths and abilities. Study your books, plan your strategies, do everything you know how to do. But you'll still be leaning on the arm of the flesh! Nothing you try will work. None of your efforts will bring you one moment of victory!"

Marshall Applewhite, the leader of the Heaven's Gate cult that committed mass suicide in March of 1997, had expected to be taken on a space ship to a "higher level" of existence. I ask you—why would anyone ever believe such a fantasy? I believe there was a very tragic reason behind it all.

This man grew up the son of a Presbyterian minister. As an adult, he became active in the church himself, serving as a choir director. He got married, had two children and was considered a wonderful family man by all who knew him. But Applewhite had a problem that wouldn't go away—a strong homosexual drive.

He lived with guilt, fear and condemnation, all raging inside him. He consulted doctors and psychiatrists, saying his urge was a "beast" that had total control over him. He even checked himself into a hospital once, in the hope of being "cured." This man tried everything he could to rid himself of his desires. But nothing ever brought him deliverance.

Years later, after Applewhite had left his family, he started a group called "The Overcomers." This group taught sexual abstinence, and Applewhite hoped that the kind of lifestyle they preached would free him. But it never did. One news account said he eventually castrated himself in order to "evict" his demon. Of the thirty-eight others who died in the Heaven's Gate suicide, one-third had submitted to castration in a desperate attempt to find freedom from the dominion of "sin."

We may be repulsed by Applewhite's cultic practices and the mass suicide he orchestrated. But, sadly, multitudes of Christians today also fight losing battles against life-controlling habits and lusts. Sin has taken dominion over many in the church, even those who weep and plead for deliverance. Their cry is loud and clear: **"O wretched man that I am! Who shall deliver me from the body of this death?"** (Romans 7:24). **"...what I hate, that I do"** (verse 15).

The more I study God's word, the clearer it becomes to me: All human striving for deliverance from sin is doomed to fail. And God will let us go through the wringer time after time, until we're totally convinced we must die to all efforts of the flesh.

When Israel attempted to defeat their powerful enemy through human power, God immediately denounced the effort: "...both he that helpeth shall fall, and he that is holpen shall fall down, and they all shall fail together" (Isaiah 31:3). God's word declares in very clear language that all victory depends on him alone. Only he has the power to deliver us from our enemies.

You may have a godly will, a solid moral background, an unpolluted mind. In fact, you may be one of the cleanest people walking this earth. But none of these things is an effective weapon when it comes to battling the powers of hell. The Bible says none of your human gifts or abilities will ever work against the devil. You will always fail by your own efforts!

ISAIAH MAKES IT CLEAR— OUR ENEMIES WILL NEVER BE DEFEATED BY THE SWORD OF MAN!

If you are in the midst of an overwhelming struggle, you must learn the word God gave to Zechariah: **"...Not by might, nor by power, but by my Spirit, saith the Lord"** (Zechariah 4:6). Your victory will never come through the sword of man—not even your own sword!

Isaiah writes: **"Then shall the Assyrian fall with the sword, not of a mighty man; and the sword, not of a mean man, shall devour him: but he shall flee from the sword, and his young men shall be discomfited"** (Isaiah 31:8). The prophet is saying a sword will indeed defeat the Assyrians. But what kind of sword will this be, if not Israel's?

In the book of Revelation, the apostle John mentions a holy sword of the Lord: **"And out of his mouth goeth a sharp sword, that with it he should smite the nations..."** (Revelation 19:15). John is speaking of Christ here, saying, "A piercing, victorious sword will come out of our Lord's mouth!"

By associating this sword with Christ's mouth, John is saying that our effective weapon in battle against all our enemies will be the voice of the Lord. Indeed, this is the very image Isaiah uses to describe how God will overthrow the Assyrians: **"For through the voice of the Lord shall the Assyrian be beaten down, which smote with a rod"** (Isaiah 30:31).

Isaiah is saying, "Your Lord promises to fight for you. He will make his voice known, and it will put all your enemies to chase!" **"The Lord shall cause his glorious voice to be heard, and shall shew the lighting down of his arm, with the indignation of his anger, and with the flame of a devouring fire, with scattering, and tempest, and hailstones"** (verse 30).

Next, Isaiah uses the image of birds to illustrate God's protective power over his people: "As birds flying, so will the Lord of hosts defend Jerusalem; defending also he will deliver it; and passing over he will preserve it" (31:5). The Hebrew meaning of this verse is, "As the hen-birds flutter over their young, so shall Jehovah, God of hosts, spread out his wings over Jerusalem."

God was telling Israel, "If you want to be protected from the onslaught of the enemy, then hide under my wings. I will secure you, covering you the way a mother hen covers her chicks. You don't have to live in fear of your enemies any longer!"

Let me ask you: Are (you) in a great warfare right now? Are you facing an enemy that is too powerful for you? If so, how do you expect to remain pure, faithful, Christlike, while others around you are falling left and right? How will you gain victory over your lusts and temptations, when Satan comes against you like a roaring lion?

God asks simply that you lay down your sword—and that you trust him to take up his sword on your behalf. He wants you to come to the point where you say, "Lord, I know the battle is not mine anymore. I've failed so many times. Now I come to you in simple faith. Help me, God. Deliver me from these overwhelming foes!"

GOD LET ISRAEL DO THINGS THEIR OWN WAY—AND THEY FAILED!

Egypt never responded to Israel's request for help. That once-mighty nation had become a broken reed. Meanwhile, Sennacherib and the Assyrian army had surrounded Jerusalem. And at that point, Hezekiah decided, "We're not going to lean on the arm of the flesh this time. We're going to do it all God's way!"

The king immediately humbled himself and sought God in prayer: **"And it came to pass, when king Hezekiah heard it, that he rent his clothes, and covered himself with sackcloth, and went into the house of the Lord"** (Isaiah 37:1). Hezekiah confessed, "Lord, I know I have nothing of myself to give you, except my faith. I can't fight Sennacherib. I'm helpless in my own strength. It all has to come from you, Lord. So, what should we do now? We're surrounded by our enemies. Please, give us your direction!"

Hezekiah knew that Isaiah would have God's word of guidance. So this time he sent his envoy to the prophet. These men said to Isaiah, **"...the children are come to the birth, and there is not strength to bring forth"** (verse 3). In other words: "This time we want to do everything God's way. But you've got to know, we're totally weak. Our defenses are depleted, with no strength left. What should we do?"

Isaiah did have God's word for them. The prophet said, **"...Be not afraid of the words that thou hast heard...I will cause (Sennacherib) to fall by the sword..."** (verses 6-7). God was saying, "Any enemy of yours is an enemy of mine now—because you have turned the battle over to me! If anyone talks against you, hurts you or abuses you, it is an attack against me. And I will take care of that enemy, whether human or demonic!"

"...He shall not come into this city, nor shoot an arrow there, nor come before it with shields, nor cast a bank against it" (verse 33). God says, "Others may be falling all around you, but that doesn't mean a thing. You are walking in covenant with me. And I have promised to do battle against every enemy that assails you!"

I think God must have an incredible sense of humor—because he sent just one angel to put the entire Assyrian army to flight. Scripture says, **"Then the angel of the Lord went forth, and smote in the camp of the Assyrians a hundred and fourscore and five thousand: and when they arose early in the morning, behold, they were all dead corpses"** (verse 36).

What an amazing sight that must have been. That morning, the Assyrians awoke to find 185,000 of their fellow soldiers slain—yet not a mark was found on any of them. And it all happened because the Israelites merely humbled themselves and sought God!

The Bible tells us the Assyrians quickly hightailed it out of Judah: **"So Sennacherib king of Assyria departed…"** (verse 37). Yet, not only were Israel's enemies scattered, but God made sure they were destroyed as well. Scripture tells us that soon afterward, Sennacherib was slain by his own two sons while worshiping in his pagan temple (see verse 38).

What a wonderful picture God has given us of his power to deliver us from our enemies in our flesh. The enemy may shoot fiery arrows at us, but they will not strike. Satan may noisily attack us with a huge army of lusts and temptations, but in the end he will turn and run. God has declared, "I will defend every child of mine who believes in me enough to lay down his own sword!"

Dear saint, the Lord is urging you: "Cling to me in the midst of your battle. Your victory is all a matter of faith in God's power and willingness to deliver you. When the enemy has overwhelmed you, come to me and pour out your soul. Seek me with all your heart, and I will do battle for you. I'll protect you as you walk in covenant with me. Your part is simply to humble yourself, truly believe in my covenant promises and seek my face. Then you will receive my word of direction. And you will see all your enemies put to flight. Your only way to full and complete victory is to <u>faith</u> your way out of your crisis!"

The battle is never ours. It is always the Lord's. Faith and faith alone—faith in God's promise to keep you from falling, to put in you a will to want to do right—this is the way to glorious freedom.

—David Wilkerson died in 2011. He was the founding pastor of Times Square Church in New York City, where he ministered to gang members and drug addicts. In 1971, he founded World Challenge, Inc., which supports missionaries and outreaches throughout the world.

Reprinted by permission: World Challenge, Inc., PO Box 260, Lindale, TX 75771. http://worldchallenge.org

IF THE CLOTHES FIT—WEAR THEM!

1. Who gives us our armor and for what purpose?

2. List the separate pieces of armor, define in our own words what each piece represents to you.

3. As Christians, we have enlisted in God's army and we are given "new uniforms" to wear. In order to wear our new uniform correctly we may need to take off our "old uniform." What type of uniform would Satan dress us in? List some specifics; e.g. instead of shoes of the gospel of peace, he would give us shoes of strife or anxiety.

4. Read **Romans 13:12-14.** What are we instructed to do? How does this compare to **Ephesians 6:10-18?** What is our part?

LESSON 6

STAYING FIT

MAIN PRINCIPLE

In Christ, we are strong. We need to keep our strength by maintaining our relationship with God through prayer, meditation on Scripture, worship and fellowship. As we learn to recognize the schemes of Satan, we will become proficient at resisting them in the power of the Spirit.

WHERE EVIL SPIRITS ROAM

by Paul Yongii Cho

HOW TO KNOW AND AVOID THEM IN YOUR LIFE AND THE LIVES OF OTHERS.

Christians have long been aware of the influence of evil spirits, strategically placed by Satan. We have confronted them with deliverance, exorcism and prayer. And with the popularity of Frank Peretti's novel This Present Darkness, we have been alerted to the reality of the spiritual battle in which we are engaged.

Paul Yonggi Cho is pastor of the world's largest church, the 600,000-member Yoido Full Gospel congregation in Seoul, South Korea. He too has long been aware of the warring that takes place in the spiritual realm. In understanding the Holy Spirit and His spiritual gifts, Cho has seen great victories in South Korea, including the establishment of 50,000 cell groups, and in his meetings around the world, including a ministry in Japan.

In his new book, The Holy Spirit, My Senior Partner, he writes: "Every morning when I awake I greet the Holy Spirit and invite Him to go with me through the day and take the lead in all my affairs, and He does. I say, 'Good morning, Holy Spirit. Let's work together today. I will be Your vessel.' Every evening before retiring I say again, 'It's been a wonderful day working with You, Holy Spirit.' "

Through this intimate walk with the Holy Spirit, Cho has learned to listen and obey. He has also learned to discern evil spirits and to understand how they affect people. Here he shares those insights in a practical, straightforward article. This teaching is taken from his book The Holy Spirit, My Senior Partner. The book also includes his personal testimony.

Two spiritual forces surround us. Because of Jesus' great love for His redeemed ones, He has sent the Holy Spirit and many angels commanding them "to minister for them who shall be heirs of salvation" (Heb. 1:14).

Not only is the Holy Spirit with us always, but many angels are also with us always. On the other hand, the enemy, Satan, who is the prince of the power of the air, is continually devising a sinister plot "to steal, and to kill, and to destroy" by sending evil and unclean spirits who walk around in the world (John 10:10). As the apostle John says, "And we know that we are of God, and the whole world lieth in wickedness" (1 John 5:19).

Seeing that these facts are true, I have come to realize that believers should discern these spirits. If you don't have the special gift of discerning the spirits, discern the work of evil spirits by following the teaching of Christ.

Jesus teaches in Matthew 7:15-20: "Beware of false prophets, which come to you in sheep's clothing, but inwardly they are ravening wolves. Ye shall know them by their fruits. Do men gather grapes of thorns, or figs of thistles? Even so every good tree bringeth forth good fruit; but a corrupt tree bringeth forth evil fruit. A good tree cannot bring forth evil fruit, neither can a corrupt tree bring forth good fruit. Every tree that bringeth not forth good fruit is hewn down, and cast into the fire. Wherefore by their fruits ye shall know them."

Even though you may have a fantastically wonderful experience or inspiration, if the fruit you bear is not in line with the Word of God and the fruit of the Holy Spirit, it can never be work that was born of the Spirit of God.

Jesus also warns: "Many will say to me in that day, Lord, Lord, have we not prophesied in thy name? and in thy name have cast out devils? and in thy name done many wonderful works? And then will I profess unto them, I never

May 1989, Charisma

knew you: depart from me, ye that work iniquity" (Matt. 7:22,23).

You should never assume merely on the basis of its supernatural aspects that any work that is followed by signs and wonders is performed as the work of God. You should always look at the fruit of or the true nature behind the work. Though the devil comes in sheep's clothing, he can neither hide nor falsify his character. Let us examine the fruits of the devil.

The Bible teaches that "the kingdom of God is…righteousness, and peace, and joy in the Holy Ghost" (Rom. 14:17). But when Satan comes in, disguised as the Holy Spirit, he steals away a person's love, joy and peace.

James 3:14-18 gives us a clear standard of judgment: "But if ye have bitter envying and strife in your hearts, glory not, and lie not against the truth. This wisdom descendeth not from above, but is earthly, sensual, devilish. For where envying and strife is, there is confusion and every evil work. But the wisdom that is from above is first pure, then peaceable, gentle, and easy to be intreated, full of mercy and good fruits, without partiality, and without hypocrisy. And the fruit of righteousness is sown in peace of them that make peace."

Those who are depressed by the spirit of the devil feel a strong interference in everything. It can be so great that the person begins to wonder, *If this is the Holy Spirit, how can He act so frivolously and prompt such thoughtless action?*

At times, the spirit of the devil tries to give instructions that imitate pretty well the Holy Spirit. These are not only about petty things but also about problems of faith.

The evil spirits also spread negativism and anxiety. In short, evil spirits continue unceasingly to send troublesome prophetic interference.

Clear words in Isaiah teach us about being associated with familiar spirits: "And when they shall say unto you, Seek unto them that have familiar spirits, and unto wizards that peep, and that mutter: should not a people seek unto their God? for the living to the dead?" (Is. 8:19).

Believers who go around making jabbering and muttering prophecies probably have familiar spirits, and they should be stopped. Prophecy from the Holy Spirit comes as God needs to speak His message to His people. It comes gently and is divinely accompanied by deep feelings of confirmation and assurance that the message was truly from God.

In many places, the Bible calls spirits "unclean" (see Matt. 10:1; Mark 1:27; Luke 6:18). Unclean spirits, the spirit of the devil, raise ugly imaginations continually against one's own will. They stick like a burr in one's heart, unlike an occasional passing thought. Sometimes unclean spirits cause people to have bad thoughts when they read the Bible. Sometimes they make one feel sick when in the presence of Spirit-filled believers. Those who are oppressed by unclean spirits are in agony, with lewd and filthy imaginations overflowing like a cesspool. When they hear the Word of God, uncontrollable false charges will afflict their hearts and arrogant thinking will rise as a snake raises its head.

Luke 6:18 says that these unclean spirits can "vex." The Holy Spirit of God brings joy, peace and a refreshing, but evil spirits bring agony and trouble to mind and body.

Though you may believe that you have received the Holy Spirit, if you are in continual agony, fear and trouble, if you always feel pressed down by a big burden, this is the sign that you are oppressed by evil spirits.

No matter how deceitfully the devil may disguise himself, when you see such fruit, you can know that his true character is like a ravening wolf.

The most important question in discerning spirits is, What does one say about Christ?

Other discrepancies in doctrine do not reach the point of life and death. But false teaching about the saving grace of Jesus Christ brings eternal destruction to those who preach it and those who hear and follow it.

The apostle John writes in 1 John 4:1-3: "Beloved, believe not every spirit, but try the spirits whether they are of God: because many false prophets are gone out into the world. Hereby know ye the Spirit of God: Every spirit that confesseth that Jesus Christ is come in the flesh is of God: And every spirit that confesseth not that Jesus Christ is come in the flesh is not of God: and this is that spirit of antichrist, whereof ye have heard that it should come; and even now already is it in the world."

Though someone insists that he has received the fullness of the Holy Spirit, though someone prophesies wonderful things and does mighty acts, if he does not claim that Jesus Christ was born of a virgin and was crucified for the redemption of the whole world, he is not of Christ. If he does not claim that Jesus Christ rose from the grave on the third day, that He ascended into heaven and sits at the right hand of the throne of God, and that He will come down in the same appearance as He was resurrected in the flesh, he does not teach by the Holy Spirit but by the spirit of antichrist.

May 1989, Charisma

Considering this, in many countries countless religious groups lead a great many people to destruction with completely false doctrines about Christ.

As familiar examples, a person may insist that he is "the Christ" and another may argue that he is "the only Lamb," threatening that unless people follow him, they are not saved. Others may contend that there is no need for Jesus to be our mediator because one can communicate directly with the Father. Because there is such a chaotic spirit in the world, we must "believe not every spirit" but strictly "try the spirits whether they are of God."

When I see believers who have latched on to a self-appointed man of grace who shows mysterious power, unconditionally following him and throwing their souls before him, I cannot help but sigh. They have not been cautious enough.

A person's speech transmits character and thought. An angry woman uses angry language. A coarse man uses vulgar language. A merciful man uses merciful language, and a good woman uses good language.

The Bible also teaches this clearly: "No man speaking by the Spirit of God calleth Jesus accursed: and no man can say that Jesus is the Lord, but by the Holy Ghost" (1 Cor. 12:3).

Therefore, when we hear a person claim to have received grace, we should listen discreetly and carefully. To discern a person's spirit, for what should we listen?

When a person who claims to have received the Holy Spirit praises himself whenever possible instead of giving glory to Jesus, he does not speak by the Spirit of Christ; he speaks by the spirit of covetousness.

The devil always shakes and rages like a serpent ready to strike, and all in an effort to show off. If a

May 1989, Charisma

person's talk honors self instead of Christ, the words are of a spirit of evil, not the Holy Spirit.

Sometimes a person who professes to have received a lot of grace will come to me and say, "Pastor, I have received much grace. The Holy Spirit told me that He loves me particularly and that He will make me a great servant by using me mightily…" If I keep listening, I often grow disgusted, because that person is not speaking words to honor Christ and God; the words are merely self-praise.

The Holy Spirit magnifies God (see Acts 10:46) and reveals the glory of Christ through us by filling us and showing us what He received of Christ (see John 16:1-14).

Whether talking privately or speaking publicly, if a person, even a servant of the Lord, shows off his own greatness, not Christ's, he is already taken by the spirit of antichrist.

When a person who professes to have received the Holy Spirit does nothing but threaten and blackmail others, when he doesn't hesitate to use coarse and hurtful language, we must be careful.

A certain sister who professed that she had received the Holy Spirit carried with her a cloud of terror instead of love and peace. If anyone corrected her, she would call down a curse. How can the personality of the Holy Spirit of God, which is meek and humble, dwell in the life of one who speaks such words?

How can that kind of person—claiming to be speaking by the Holy Spirit and favored with special blessing—knock on believer's doors, whisper slander to church members and demand hush money unscrupulously?

Before we affirm what wonderful works a person does, we must first notice if he or she praises God

and preaches Christ as the Lord. We must see evidence of humility, of a person hidden behind the cross, speaking and acting out the fruit of the Holy Spirit.

The apostle Paul warns us about believers in the latter times: "Now the Spirit speaketh expressly, that in the latter times some shall depart from the faith, giving heed to seducing spirits, and doctrines of devils" (1 Tim. 4:1).

Wherever the real thing exists, there will be counterfeits. Therefore, we should not only always examine our own spiritual experience, but also look to discerning the spirits in order to guide our fellowship with other believers.

—Paul "David" Yonggi Cho has founded and pastored the world's largest church, the Yoido Full Gospel Church in Seoul, South Korea with 830,000 members as of 2007. He pioneered the use of cell groups as a means of evangelism and church growth.

Reprinted by permission Charisma Magazine and Strang Communications Company.

HEROES OF SPIRITUAL WARFARE

by Brother Andrew

TODAY GOD IS CALLING AN ARMY INTO BATTLE -- WILL YOU JOIN HIM?

Do you know what *jihad* is? This expression is found in the Koran and is what Iran's Ayatollah Khomeini has waged on his neighbors in Iraq and other Arab countries. Many Arab countries would like to do this to Israel. *Jihad* is a "holy war"—total, all-out war.

The amazing thing is that God himself has declared *jihad*. God has declared total war against everything that stands in opposition to His holiness, His righteousness, His justice and His love. As far as He is concerned, there can never be any compromise between good and evil. God is not very diplomatic in this regard. God is a warrior, and He calls His people to spiritual battle.

Spiritual warfare is raging all around us. It's not just the house church meeting illegally in China, or Christians who are forbidden to proselytize in Muslim countries who know its reality. In fact, it's sometimes easier to stand firm and fight when war has been openly declared! But all of us face this battle.

We see it in the seductive and popular appeal of the New Age movement; in the way "responsible sex" (i.e., using contraceptives) has replaced sexual purity; in the way abortion and euthanasia have been "rephrased" to sound acceptable and compassionate; in the way "personal fulfillment" is replacing "commitment" as a priority in marriage; in the way "freedom of religion" is coming to mean "freedom *from* religion"; in the way materialism and self-interest have numbed our sensitivity to those who suffer around the world—and in our own backyard; in the way drug traffickers are leaving a trail of ruined young lives for personal profit; in the way we put our trust in a nuclear arsenal.

A battle needs heroes who are willing to put their lives on the line, and spiritual warfare needs heroes of the faith willing to do the same.

The people in the Bible whom we've called heroes of the faith—all those men and women of God who were used so mightily by Him—were people engaged in spiritual warfare. These biblical heroes seem larger than life to us today—Moses, the great emancipator! David, the king after God's own heart!—yet in their time, they were just ordinary people who were willing to stand up for the truth of God, speak the truth and act on it. And that is what we are called to do today.

But to fight this battle, we need to be equipped. We must *know* God's Word, we must *live* God's Word, we must *speak* God's Word, we must put God's Word into the hands of all people.

Anyone who stands up and boldly proclaims the Word of God today will not only have a following but, in most cases, opposition as well. That is why the need is greater than ever for people to be trained in the Word of God.

God has not equipped us to run away from conflict. If our objective were to avoid conflict with the enemy, we would never win the battle. Instead, we are to be warriors, aggressively and offensively facing the enemy, not trying to escape.

A famous Czech communist once said, "I can only honor my opponent in a debate if he makes an all-out effort to convert me." But because so few Christians are willing to stand up and openly challenge the communist philosophy with the Word of God, they despise us. We

November 1988, Charisma

do not win our opponent by refusing to debate him, but by openly confronting falsehood with truth.

This is one reason we Christians in the free world must help provide what every suffering Christian in the world needs most--a copy of the Bible. It is my mission to give the suffering church the weapon it needs to wage spiritual warfare.

Paul tells us to take up the "sword of the Spirit, which is the Word of God." All the other parts of the spiritual armor are defensive. The sword is offensive. By it we make forward progress in defeating the enemy.

The weapons God has provided for the Christian to use are not bombs and guns, not economic leverage and boycotts, not even education or diplomatic negotiations. This is because, as Paul says, "We are not contending against flesh and blood, but against principalities, against the powers, against the world rulers of this present darkness, against the spiritual hosts of wickedness in the heavenly places." Those evil forces do create tangible earthly suffering and oppression, but *the* weapon God has empowered us to use is the Sword of the Spirit, which is the Word of God.

The devil also uses weapons. To be effective warriors we must know our enemy and understand the kinds of weapons he uses. The devil's main weapon is to sow doubt in our trust of the Word of God.

Any time we try to argue with the devil on any other basis than what is written in the Word of God, we are sure to lose. The devil had thousands of years of experience with people, plenty of time to think up a confounding answer to any smart remark we might devise. We have only one effective weapon and that is the Word of God. Only that will make us heroes of the faith.

Why are so many Christians

weak and ineffective? With all of the accumulated knowledge we have of the Scriptures and church history and counseling and psychology and psychiatry and everything else, many are still trying to be heroes along paths God has not led them.

If God calls you to become a warrior, become a warrior. If God calls you to become an intercessor, become an intercessor. If God calls you to be a Bible smuggler with Open Doors, become a Bible smuggler with Open Doors. But if God calls you to raise a family for Him, or be His witness in the market place, don't try to do something else.

I remember when I was a very young Christian, my first desire was to be a missionary. I went to an old pastor in Holland and I said, "Pastor, I want to go to the mission field."

THE QUESTION IS, ARE YOU IN THE RIGHT WAY? -- THE WAY GOD HAS CHOSEN FOR YOU?

I thought he would pat me on the shoulder and say, "Good boy, Andrew" But no. With a very serious face he said, "Well, Andrew, maybe that is the only place where God can keep you from backsliding." I didn't like that message because it didn't seem to reflect a very high opinion of me. But the older I grew the more I came to agree with him. The question is, are you in the right *way*?--the way God has chosen for *you*?

God has a way for each one of us where we can become a warrior for God, and that is the only place where God can protect us.

The son of a friend of mine

is very interested in medieval history. He likes to dress up like a knight and, using wooden swords and shields, have mock battles with his friends. More than once he's come in from the backyard with a scrape or bruise from a whack with a wooden sword.

But real swords present real dangers—just like any modern weapon. A person who uses a weapon to hunt or for self-defense or in the army can be infinitely more hazardous to himself or others if he is not aware of the dangers to avoid. This is true of the Sword of the Spirit, as well.

In the Garden of Eden Eve made a mistake in the way she handled God's word. She misquoted God. When Eve quoted God's words, she added a little: "You shall not eat of the fruit of the tree which is in the midst of the garden, *neither shall you touch it, lest you die*" (Gen. 3:3, emphasis added).

It's just as dangerous to add to the Word of God as it is to take away from it. In this case, there is no record of God telling Adam and Eve not to touch the tree, so when Satan responded, "You will not die," he had the strategic advantage of a half-truth. Indeed, when Eve touched the tree, she didn't die, so why not go ahead and eat the fruit?

How many people have been turned away from the gospel when they encountered a commandment of man being preached as the Word of God? By one means or another, people always discover that the commandments of men are not true and just, and when they do, they think their discovery gives them justification to dismiss the whole gospel.

Eve may have had an excuse for misquoting God. His commandments were not yet written down. But we have no such excuse. We can turn to the Bible and see exactly what He has said or hasn't said. Therefore, we have a great responsibility to handle the Word of God properly. Think of the consequences of that first mishandling of God's Word—the whole human race fell into sin!

As we accept God's call to become a hero of the faith, each of us may wonder how we can develop the confidence to face the enemy single-handedly. In a world full of hatred, rampant sin and evil ideologies, can you go in alone and establish a work for God?

Let's first establish that going it alone is not the ideal way. God has called us into a fellowship--church congregations and ministries—and together we are part of the army of the Lord. That is why God gives different gifts to different people, so that we can work together to build up the kingdom of God. It is as Christ's body that we should move out into the world and win the world for Christ, not as individual Lone Rangers.

However, I believe it is possible to stand alone for Christ. Throughout the Scriptures we see many men and women who had to stand alone in order to accomplish something important for God by faith—just read Hebrews 11. We need to know that we *can* because there will be times when we have to stand alone—or at least it may feel that way.

We may feel like the only parents who won't let their son or daughter stay out all night—stand firm! You may feel like the only guy at work that doesn't tell dirty jokes —stand firm! You may be the only member of your family willing to give up an impressive salary to serve the poor at home or overseas—stand firm!

We need to know that God has equipped us through His Spirit and with His Word to be fully capable soldiers, fit for any combat into which He sends us. Without that confidence, our nerve won't be steady under fire. We'll be looking to the right and the left for help from others when we should be facing the enemy head-on.

Not only has God declared *jihad*, so has the devil. In Revelation we find something very interesting: "These are of one mind and give over their power and authority to the beast; they will make war on the Lamb, and the Lamb will conquer them, for He is Lord of Lords and King of Kings, and those with Him are called and chosen and faithful" (Rev. 17:13-14).

Jihad originated with God, but all the enemies of Christ temporarily unite to make war on the Lamb. They may hate each other, but their common hatred for the Lamb is greater than their hatred of each other, so together they declare *jihad* on the Lamb.

Notice that this passage in Revelation does not say that they will make war on the church as an organization. Even today there are hostile places in the world where some expressions of the church are not really persecuted. If you compromise enough, let the state regulate your activities, don't evangelize

///

IF YOU ARE PERSECUTED, REJOICE! IT IS JUST ABOUT THE SUREST PROOF THAT THE SON OF GOD LIVES IN YOU; OTHERWISE YOU WOULDN'T BE PERSECUTED.

///

or make any waves, then there is the possibility of continuing to function without much persecution.

The Lamb of God is Satan's ultimate target. And it's the life of Christ in the believer and in the church—*Christ in you*—that is the target of persecutions.

Unfortunately, some Christians unwittingly play right into Satan's battle scheme, like a basketball player that sinks a shot into the opponent's basket. When "big name" Christians fight and quarrel with each other over public airwaves, the Lamb of God is wounded. When a church ignores its needy neighbors, it is Christ that is ignored. When Christian organizations mismanage their funds, Christ's name is defiled. When Christians drag other Christians into court, it is Christ that is judged.

I'm so glad the battle doesn't stop there. I'm glad we can know the end of the story, because the Lamb does overcome. Scripture doesn't say that the enemy will break his teeth when he tries to chew on a passive Lamb. No. The Lamb will also fight! There is a spiritual war going on in which every individual Christian is invited to take part. And we can fight in confidence because we know who wins! The Lamb overcomes because He is Lord of Lords and King of Kings, and those who are with Him are the called and chosen and faithful.

This, then, is the message that we have for the suffering church worldwide: If you are persecuted, rejoice! It is just about the surest proof that the Son of God lives in you; otherwise you wouldn't be persecuted.

Most problems in the world are not political issues but spiritual. It's a battle for the minds and hearts of men and women. The enemy lies, intimidates, misquotes Scripture, or

November 1988, Charisma

invents a new religion with a different "holy book." The only answer is to rightly handle the Word of Truth which can make people free as individuals, and make nations free.

People need to know what scriptures say, but to do this they must have access to the Word of God for study and meditation. That's why it is so important to make the Word of God available to every nation in the world. No military assistance, no diplomatic power, no economic aid or food we give to any nation is going to make a basic difference in the world situation because it does not change the attitude of people toward life, toward sin, toward the devil, and toward God.

Horace Greeley, the famous American communicator and leader in the antislavery movement during the last century, made a marvelous statement: "It is impossible to enslave mentally or socially a Bible-reading people." The principles of the Bible are the groundwork of human freedom. If we make the Word of God available, no evil ideology, no strange philosophy, no idolatrous religion can effectively take hold of any people in a permanent way. The Bible is the only book that does not need a defense; it has stood the test for centuries; it continues to change lives. It has the words of eternal life.

Exodus 15 records the Song of Moses, and in it is the line "The Lord is a man of war; the Lord is His name" (Ex. 15:3). Interestingly, when we go to the end of the Bible, we find in Revelation 15:3 that the conquering saints are still singing the Song of Moses. Throughout this entire age, until evil has been completely banished, the Lord is identified as a man of war, standing in the gap, calling people to follow His example and do likewise.

The battle is all around us; are you feeling afraid? Look up— Christ goes before you, accompanied by many heroes of the faith who have gone before. Learn from their example. Pick up the Sword of the Spirit, learn to use it well, bring its light into the dark places, strike down falsehood with truth. Let us heed God's call to become heroes of the faith, so that we can say with the apostle Paul, "I have fought the good fight, I have finished the race, I have kept the faith" (2 Tim. 4:7).

—Reprinted from *A Time for Heroes,* copyright 1988, by Brother Andrew. Published by Servant Publications, Ann Arbor, Michigan. Used with permission

Brother Andrew, born in the Netherlands in 1928, is known for taking Bibles to persecuted believers and was nicknamed "God's Smuggler." He is the founder of the ministry Open Doors, which reaches the suffering church worldwide. His books include *God's Smuggler* and *What Happens When Muslims Believe in Christ.*

WHO DOES THE FIGHTING?

Some Scriptures indicate that we fight:

1. **1 Timothy 1:18–19**—

2. **1 Timothy 6:12**—

3. **1 Corinthians 9:26–27 (See AMP)**—

4. **Psalm 144:1**—

5. **Nehemiah 4:14–23**—

Some Scriptures indicate that the <u>Lord</u> fights for us:

1. **Nehemiah 4:20**—

2. **Exodus 14:13–14**—

3. **Deuteronomy 1:29–30; 3:22; 20:1–4**—

4. **2 Chronicles 32:7–8**—

5. **Jeremiah 1:18-19**

LESSON 7

WARFARE IN THE HEAVENLIES

MAIN PRINCIPLE

We are seated with Christ in heavenly places far above all rule and authority, power and dominion. God has given us the ministry of angels to help and protect us. In prayer, we can appropriate their help in the spiritual realm to accomplish what God has called us to do.

ANGELS ALL AROUND

by Terry Law

HEAVEN'S MESSENGERS ARE STILL VERY PRESENT TODAY— AIDING AND PROTECTING THE SAINTS.

It seems everyone has an angel story today. Books about sightings and interactions with angels are selling like wildfire. At least 50 books on the subject are scheduled for release by February 1995. *Time, Newsweek* and even the *Wall Street Journal* have run articles on angels.

Unfortunately, few of these stories seem to apply any standard for measuring whether people are seeing angels, demonic beings appearing as angels or figments of their imaginative minds. Few accounts correlate with biblical data, and many have an obvious New Age flavor.

As Christians, it is important for us to distinguish between the false and the true. The fact is that despite the deception and misinformation rampant in the current plethora of angel sightings, the Bible says that angels are real.

There is practical, biblical teaching about the role God has given angels in our lives. As the psalmist wrote, "For He shall give His angels charge over you, to keep you in all your ways" (Ps. 91:11, NKJV). By applying biblical standards, we can distinguish between angels sent by God and those evil beings masquerading as angels "of light" (see 2 Cor. 11:14).

Many of the historical reports about angels, especially from war times, include incidents in which seemingly miraculous events occurred. The details without natural explanation often are attributed to angelic intervention.

Some of these stories involve nations; some involve individuals. Some have more than one witness who saw the same thing or similar things.

Several of the most well-known interventions during war involve the periods when Great Britain and the Allies were in opposition to the German powers. Angels appear to have intervened on behalf of the Allies more than once. These stories have appeared in print many times before, but they bear repeating.

Does the fact that angels intervened on behalf of the Allies mean all of the people in the Central or Axis nations were against God? Of course not. However, the people in those countries were under ungodly governmental authorities—particularly in World War II Germany.

The ruling Nazi party was very opposed to God. We hear and read frequently about Hitler's intention to wipe out the Jews. Consequently, any Christian who was caught withstanding the Nazis or aiding the Jews was killed or put in a concentration camp.

God does not "take sides," but He helps those who are on His side. And He does pull down evil kingdoms (see Jer. 18:7-8).

ANGELS IN WORLD WAR I

A story from World War I, known as The Angels of Mons, was told throughout England within a month after it occurred. Of all wartime reports about angels, the incident at Mons probably has the most witnesses who reported similar sightings.

Near Mons, France, in August 1914, heavily outnumbered British troops had fought with no respite for days. They had lost many men, and defeat looked inevitable.

Captain Cecil W. Hayward reported how, suddenly, in the midst of a gun battle, firing on both sides stopped. To their astonishment, the British troops saw "four or five wonderful beings, much bigger than men" between themselves and the Germans.

These "men" were bare-headed, wore white robes and seemed to float rather than stand. Their backs were to the British and their arms and hands were outstretched toward the Germans. At that moment, the horses of the German cavalrymen became terrified and stampeded off in every direction.

Hayward told of another battle sometime later in World War I when matters again seemed hopeless for British soldiers who were surrounded by German troops. Suddenly, the heavy German fire stopped, and everything grew strangely quiet. The sky then opened "with a bright shining light, and figures of luminous beings appeared," floating between the British and German lines.

German troops retreated in disorder, allowing the Allied forces to re-form and fall back to a line of defense. When German prisoners taken that day were asked why they surrendered when they had the British troops surrounded, they looked amazed and said, "But there were hosts and hosts of you."

Author Hope Price, who recorded these and many other stories in her book Angels (Macmillan/London), says she believes that Britain's commitment to pray on national days of prayer is what brought the angelic intervention on behalf of British soldiers.

In effect, the official government of a nation represents that nation. Actions of the government bring divine intervention, it seems, both for blessing and judgment.

ANGELS IN WORLD WAR II

One Sunday morning in September 1940, Prime Minister Winston Churchill and some military advisers were in an underground operations room in southern England watching the lights on the electrical battle charts. Britain suffered from a dangerous shortage of materials, and intelligence reports showed German forces were preparing to invade England.

On that otherwise quiet Sunday morning, a sudden alert heralded the approach of about 200 Nazi aircraft. As outnumbered British air squadrons rose to meet the Nazi formations nearing the English coast, tension grew in the underground shelter.

"Then inexplicably, the discs [markers] on the

wall chart began to move eastward," writes Katherine Pollard Carter in her book Mighty Hand of God (Impact Christian Books). "The great Nazi air flotilla had turned back. With 185 of their aircraft downed in flames, they were in retreat! Miraculously, against all logistical probability, the Royal Air Force had won the battle!"

There was no natural explanation for the outcome of this Nazi attack during the Battle of Britain, but intelligence officers who interrogated captured Nazi airmen heard this question from at least three different men: "Where did you get all the planes you threw into the battle over Britain?" Apparently, the Germans saw many more planes than the British actually had in the air.

The explanation? Again, the British as a nation were praying for the safety of their country and their military forces. From 1940 to the end of the war, people throughout the British Commonwealth observed a silent moment of prayer every day at 9 p.m.

As Carter records, one imprisoned Nazi intelligence officer told his captors: "With the striking of your Big Ben clock each evening at nine, you used a secret weapon which we did not understand. It was very powerful, and we could find no countermeasure against it."

Evangelist Billy Graham relates an incident, which reportedly occurred during the Battle of Britain, in his book Angels: God's Secret Agents (Word). He quotes a story by reporter Adela Rogers St. John of a postwar celebration attended by Lord Hugh Dowding, along with the king and many other dignitaries.

Lord Dowding told of British pilots who were badly wounded or even dead in their cockpits -- yet their planes kept flying. On occasion, other pilots saw figures at the controls who were not RAF pilots. Lord Dowding believed angels actually piloted those planes.

Roy Hicks Sr., in his book Guardian Angels (Harrison House), writes about U.S. Army chaplain Alex B. Cowie, who was stationed in the Pacific during World War II. Cowie was riding in a military transport plane when it was attacked by Japanese fighter planes. "We're going down," the pilot told him.

The chaplain began to pray, and as he looked out the window, records Hicks, "the Lord opened his eyes, and he saw a mighty angel holding up the wing of the plane. He looked out the other side and saw another angel holding up that wing."

After they landed, Cowie said, everyone who saw the damage to the plane marveled that it had made it back with everyone safe.

OTHER ANGELIC RESCUES

November 1994, Charisma

Carter reports two other instances of angelic rescues in her book. One, which occurred in early 1968, involved an entire village in South Vietnam.

Cliff Custer told this story in May 1968 at Oral Roberts University during the annual meeting of Camps Farthest Out.

Along with his friend Keith Swaggerty, Custer was visiting a Vietnamese village where there were many Christians. A Viet Cong soldier—man who lived in that community as a youth—slipped in to warn the villagers that they would be attacked the next day by 1,000 Viet Cong.

The villagers had no weapons or ammunition, and only a few men could fight. They decided to let the Lord be their defender. Instead of trying to escape or hide in fear, they prayed fervently and sang songs of praise and thanksgiving that filled their hearts "with a strange peace and courage," Custer said.

The next night, the first shots were heard. But then, just as suddenly, the firing stopped. There was nothing but silence for the rest of the night and the following day. A few days later, some of the Viet Cong were captured by South Vietnamese forces and brought into the village.

"Why did you halt your attack on our village?" they were asked.

"As we opened fire," the Viet Cong prisoners replied, "suddenly there appeared all around the village men clad in shining white. We fired at them, but they wouldn't fall. They shone brighter than the sun, and we couldn't aim at them. We were terrified, and we ran."

Carter also reports that during the Boxer Rebellion in China in 1900, missionaries of several denominations in and around Peking fled to the British Embassy. During one attack, the missionaries saw their enemy abruptly stop and point upward. Suddenly, the attacking force fled.

Chinese who were captured said: "We saw the walls suddenly swarming with angels in white. Everyone began shouting that the *shen* [gods] had come down to fight for the foreigners and our cause was lost."

In his book, *God, Satan and Angels* (Word of Grace), John MacArthur Jr. tells of another missionary story involving a man named John Paton. One night, natives known to be cannibals surrounded the lean-to on the South Pacific beach where Paton and his wife were living.

The couple dropped to their knees and prayed. Soon the attackers vanished into the jungle.

A year later, the chief of the tribe was converted and Paton asked him why the group left so hurriedly

that night. The chief described seeing "hundreds of big men" in shining clothes with swords in their hands.

JUST COINCIDENCE?

Some may think the connection between prayer and angelic assistance or other miracles is just a coincidence, but as William Temple, the late archbishop of Canterbury, once pointed out, "When I pray, coincidences happen; and when I do not, they don't."

We shouldn't be surprised to hear of angelic interventions in times of battle. As C.S. Lewis wrote in his classic book *Mere Christianity*, "[God] has all eternity in which to listen to the split second of prayer put up by a pilot as his plane crashes in flames."

As the Bible clearly relates, the earnest prayers of people who cry out to God often bring deliverance. And, at times, that deliverance is in the form of angelic ministry.

The fact is that God has an overall plan for this planet and for His children. If human events directly affect His plan, you may be sure that angels will be involved.

—Adapted from *The Truth About Angels* by Terry Law, copyright 1994. Published by Creation House, Orlando, Florida Used by permission.

Terry Law led his first missionary trip behind the Iron Curtain in 1968. Since then, his ministry of evangelism and worship has taken him throughout the former Soviet Union and to more than 40 countries with his Living Sound music teams. He is the president and founder of World Compassion/ Terry Law Ministries and Living Sound International in Tulsa, Oklahoma.

November 1994, Charisma

WINNING THE BATTLE FOR THE NEIGHBORHOOD

by John Dawson

HOW YOU CAN DRIVE AWAY THE DEMON FORCES NOW DOMINATING THE STREETS WHERE YOU LIVE.

I sat on the platform with other preachers listening as Paul Yonggi Cho, pastor of Yoido Full Gospel Church in Seoul, Korea, spoke to the crowd about spiritual warfare. As he testified about a hair-raising personal confrontation with an evil spirit, the Holy Spirit turned my thoughts toward the ministry of Jesus recorded in the Gospels. Jesus seems to have been in constant confrontation with demons. He regularly discerned their presence and their work.

As I reflected on Jesus' spiritual warfare, I asked myself, When was the last time I truly exercised the gift of discernment in relation to my circumstances? I always prayerfully exercise the authority of the believer in resisting the enemy when I minister, and from time to time, I rebuke the demonic forces that I sense in a particular circumstance. But was I really seeing all that the Holy Spirit could reveal to me?

I knew that exercising the gifts of the Spirit had a lot to do with personal initiative. Our will is involved, so I asked Jesus for His view of the unseen realm in my home, my office and my ministry. "Lord, do I have blind spots?" I asked. "Are there subtle influences of demonic accusation and deception that I am totally unaware of?"

All the way home on the plane I pondered this question and turned attentively to the still, small voice of the Holy Spirit. Because I travel extensively as a Bible teacher, many people pray for me. Two intercessors in different cities had recently told me that a spirit of accusation was attempting to destroy my family and ministry. *What did that really mean? How should I come against it? I can't become paranoid about demons,* I thought.

Some people see deliverance as the solution for everything, when the problem really should be solved through repentance, proper management or application of some other principle. "Well, Lord," I said, "if there is an actual demon attacking me I trust that You will show me."

The plane landed. I retrieved my baggage and flagged down my wife as she circled the Los Angeles airport in our family van. As soon as the door opened I sensed it. I felt the oppression of an evil spirit right in the van with my wife and three sons -- not possessing anybody, just lurking in the background.

As we drove out of the airport I thought back over the last six months. There was definitely a pattern of criticism and misunderstanding in some of our external family relationships. I drove into a parking lot and explained to my family what I was feeling. I said what we had gone through was more than the expected stress of a busy life. There was an insidious pattern of harassment that became clearer the more we discussed it. As the priest in my home, I joined with my wife in commanding the spirit to go from us. Immediately we sensed the departure of an evil presence.

The next day I prayed earnestly for my staff at the Los Angeles Youth With a Mission headquarters. As I prayed, a picture of the board room came into my mind. The directors meet in this room to seek the Lord and to make long-range decisions. In my mind's eye,

April 1990, Charisma

I could see a gloomy cloud hovering in a corner next to the ceiling. I understood that I was discerning a spirit of unbelief.

Yes, that's it, I thought. Every time we meet in there, everybody becomes unusually anxious about finances, even though God has proved so faithful.

I suddenly became angry—angry at a spirit that would dare to accuse our generous, faithful, heavenly Father.

During the next few days, we experienced a season of spiritual housecleaning. A spirit of confusion that had oppressed a family for months was exposed and sent into the waste places (Matt. 12:43) along with several other demons that had been practicing a subtle harassment right in the middle of our Christian ministry.

It is no surprise that I was discovering demonic activity at a Youth With a Mission base. Any effective ministry is going to be the subject of satanic attack.

Satan is a religious spirit who hangs around religious leaders and institutions. He has only two weapons: to accuse and to deceive. He hurls his accusations and lies with greatest effect in the religious world.

What do we see Satan doing in the Bible? Accusing Job (Job 1), deceiving Eve (Gen. 3), accusing the saints before the throne of God (Rev. 12:10), and tempting Jesus with a kingdom without the cross (Matt. 4:1-11). The devil built the temptations of Jesus on a subtle accusation of the character of God the Father.

Satan is not omnipresent. Where do you think he is right now? I think he's probably trying to accuse and deceive the Christian leader who is most threatening to his kingdom. High-ranking spirits oppress Christian leaders as in the

incident of delayed revelation recorded in the life story of Daniel. Daniel was kept from a God-given revelation because the territorial spirit over Persia withstood a messenger angel for 21 days until the archangel Michael joined the fight (Dan. 10).

Most believers are well taught on the authority of the believer and the gifts of the Spirit. What I have just described is not an attempt to go over that ground again but to remind us to be vigilant.

Let me ask you the question that I asked myself that day as I listened to Pastor Cho: When was the last time you truly exercised the gift of discernment in relation to your circumstances?
Before you answer that question, remember some basics:

- The gifts of the Spirit are simply the abilities of Jesus, just as the fruit of the Spirit represents the personality of Jesus.

- Jesus lives in you, the believer, and He is able to be in you and through you everything you are not.

- He is the source of our victory over sin, our wisdom, strength, love and power.

- He doesn't give us some truth. He *is* truth and He lives His life through us as we yield to His control.

One of the abilities or gifts of Jesus' Holy Spirit within us is the ability to discern or see the activity of spirits in the unseen realm (1 Cor. 12:10). We can choose to exercise this gift or neglect it even though we believe it is biblical.

Sometimes we think that the gifts of the Spirit are the special

domain of "super-mature" Christians, but the truth is that they are part of God's grace expressed in order to bring all of us to maturity. You can and should stir up this gift within you. It may not be your special ministry emphasis, but discernment should not be neglected in your daily life.

But, you might ask, how do I exercise a gift? First let's look at a gift often expressed or witnessed by Christians—the gift of prophecy. Many believers have been used by the Holy Spirit to impart a special word of encouragement to other believers in a home meeting or church service. When this occurs it is not a result of the Holy Spirit's grabbing the person and forcing speech from his lips. The person usually senses the beginning of what God wants to say and voluntarily yields to the Holy Spirit in expressing that thought. He begins in faith out of love for God and His people, and as thought follows thought the prophecy moves to completion.

Exercising discernment is a similar experience in that it is an act of the will and an act of faith. It takes a childlike humility to act upon the impressions that the Holy Spirit brings us.

I feel very vulnerable telling you the introductory story for this article because I have departed from the safe ground of the tangible and exposed to you the highly subjective experience of my inner life with God. This kind of unsophisticated vulnerability is needed if we are to see any supernatural manifestation of the Lord's power. Signs and wonders follow steps of obedience to the Master's voice.

According to the Bible our lives are lived in the midst of an invisible spiritual war. One of the most dangerous things we can do is simply to ignore this reality. We accept the Bible as true but we often live as though the battle existed on some far-off mission field, not here in our city. The fact is, there is a battle raging over your city and it is affecting you right now. Our individual blind spots and vices are usually common to the culture around us, and that culture is influenced by what the Bible calls principalities and powers (Eph. 6:12). In other words, you are being buffeted by the same temptations as others around you.

Another thing to note is that spiritual warfare begins at a personal level and escalates through layers of increasing difficulty -- from personal and family to the realm of church life, and beyond that to the collective church in the city and the national and international realms.

Have you ever thought about the battle for your immediate neighborhood? For the last 10 years I have lived in the black community in Los Angeles. My neighbors and I have common enemies. Spirits of despair, hopelessness, depression, discouragement and rejection torment this community.

Even as I write, my neighborhood is making headlines because of gang violence and mass arrests. Much of this is explained by a history of social oppression, but we must not underestimate the spiritual implications. The Bible says that we are not fighting against flesh and blood (Eph. 6:12). The devastation of drugs and violence stems from the destruction of the family, and the destruction of the family is accelerated in an atmosphere of despair.

What creates atmosphere? Atmosphere is a theatrical term for the collective mood of an audience during a play, but in daily life the human spirit is sensitive to many unseen things in the spiritual realm. Man is, by definition, an incarnate spirit and is sensitive to spiritual realities, including the activity of demons seeking to oppress and deceive.

Several years ago my staff and I went on a prayer walk around our neighborhood. We stood in front of every house, rebuked Satan in Jesus' name and prayed for a revelation of Jesus in the life of each family. We are still praying. There is a long way to go, but social, economic and spiritual transformation is evident. There were times when demonic oppression almost crushed my soul. I was often depressed at the sight of boarded-up houses, unemployed youth and disintegrating families, but I was determined not to run away.

Today there are at least nine Christian families in the block where I live, and there is a definite sense of the Lord's peace. The neighborhood is no longer disintegrating. People are renovating their houses and a sense of community is being established.

The battle is very real. Drugs are sold all night several doors down at a house belonging to an alcoholic who is unchanged after years of prayer and ministry. These realities are a challenge to my faith, but I believe that as we continue in prayer the demons of hopelessness, violence and addiction will be driven from this place completely, and my neighbors will have the opportunity to receive ministry without demonic interference.

—Excerpted from *Taking Our Cities for God* by John Dawson, copyright 1989. Creation House, Altamonte Springs, Florida. Reprinted by permission.

John Dawson has long been associated with, and served a term as president of, Youth With a Mission, an international missionary organization of Christians from many denominations dedicated to presenting Jesus Christ to this generation.

LESSON 8

ARE THERE SUCH THINGS AS TERRITORIAL SPIRITS?

MAIN PRINCIPLE

The very definition of principalities tells us that we are dealing with spirits that operate both demographically and geographically. Yet, the Church has paid little or no attention to territorial spirits! We need to ask the Holy Spirit to sharpen our ability to discern and identify such spirits so that we pray more effectively.

THE BATTLE IS THE LORD'S

by Eddie and Alice Smith

MORE CHRISTIANS ARE PRAYING THAN EVER BEFORE, BUT SOME DOWNRIGHT FLAKY THINGS ARE HAPPENING WHEN FOLKS GATHER TO CONDUCT 'SPIRITUAL WARFARE.' BEFORE YOU ENGAGE IN BATTLE WITH THE ENEMY, MAKE SURE YOU HAVE GOD'S WAR PLAN.

The atmosphere was electric. The high-energy worship time had concluded, and Eddie was introduced as the speaker for the evening. Because this was an area-wide spiritual warfare conference, the worship time had included a number of spiritual warfare songs.

Eddie took the microphone from the worship leader, tossed his Bible onto the pulpit and enthusiastically shouted, "How many people here have the power to bind Satan in the name of Jesus?"

As he expected, there was a thunderous response. Hands went up all across the city auditorium. Some, if not most, held up both hands. Many began to dance in place as the guitar played riffs and the drummer accompanied the shouting with drum rolls and cymbal crashes. The celebration went on for 30 more seconds.

When silence prevailed, Eddie leaned across the pulpit and spoke softly into the microphone: "Then would someone please do it?

Would one of you please bind Satan once and for all so we can put an end to child abuse, pornography, murder, rape, abortion, sickness, pain and all the rest? Who will volunteer?"

There were no takers.

The point? It is time for us to learn what we *can* and *cannot* do—and to establish what we should and should not do--concerning spiritual warfare. It's time for the church to grow up and understand that this is a real war with real casualties. This is not a game. It's not a charismatic shouting match.

There's far too much foolishness today when it comes to defeating darkness! The church needs discretionary warriors.

Two preachers were arguing one day. The first said, "Brother, I wouldn't be calling the devil names like that if I were you. Even Michael the archangel was careful not to insult the devil when he argued with him about the body of Moses" (see Jude 9).

The second preacher answered, "Brother, I wouldn't either if I were just an archangel. But I'm a blood-bought child of God with royal blood flowing through my veins."

Both these answers should grieve us. Certainly, as Christians we are not to be fearful. After all, we are "more than conquerors" (Rom. 8:37, NKJV). On the other hand, we are no match for an ancient being such as the devil. Even Jesus didn't respond to him arrogantly or foolishly when He was tempted in the wilderness.

Is binding Satan difficult or impossible? No. In fact, the Bible says that it will be done. "Then I saw an angel coming down from heaven, having the key to the bottomless pit and a great chain in his hand. He laid hold of the dragon, that serpent of old, who is the Devil or Satan, and bound him for a thousand years" (Rev. 20:1-2).

Notice that it isn't a "blood-bought child of God" who binds

December 1999, Charisma

Satan. It isn't even an archangel. It's just an ordinary angel to whom God will one day give a chain, a key and a command! When God wills something to be done, a toddler can do it.

The key is—*when God wills it.* Until that time, all the stomping, dancing, sword-swinging and *shofar*-blowing in the world won't bring the devil down once and for all.

Neither will your position as an intercessor. The Son of God Himself admitted that He could do nothing on His own: " 'Most assuredly, I say to you, the Son can do nothing of Himself, but what He sees the Father do; for whatever He does, the Son also does in like manner' " (John 5:19).

Discretionary warfare is warfare that involves doing only what the Father is doing—nothing *less*, nothing *more* and nothing *else*!

SPIRITUAL WARFARE FADS

Some of us still don't understand this picture. When we gather to pray, we get into all kinds of weirdness, as if the performance we put on is somehow going to shoo the devil away.

A few years ago we attended a spiritual warfare gathering in a Southern city. After two hours of warfare singing, the leader mounted the stage.

"Everyone on your feet!" he yelled with the gusto of a drill sergeant. Then more than 700 people jumped to their feet obediently.

"Now hold up your right hand!" They did.

"Now I want you to grab the Prince of Pride over our city by the tail. Get a hold of Slue Foot's slimy old tail. Have you got it?" the leader queried.

The crowd thundered, "Yes!"

"Now on the count of three we're gonna pull the Prince of Pride down out of the heavenlies. Are you ready? One, two, three, *pull!*"

The problem here was not so much with the nature of the attack—although we question whether this activity had any impact on the spiritual atmosphere of the city—as with the timing. In a spiritual battle, the air war can't begin until the ground war is finished.

But what is the ground war? It is the war within our own hearts and minds and in our relationships with one another. It is a war that is waged face down in repentance and reconciliation.

> "THE CHURCH'S GREATEST NEED IS NOT TO DECLARE WAR ON HELL BUT TO DECLARE WAR ON OUR OWN SIN."

It's neither fun nor exciting. But we cannot pull down strongholds with one hand that we support with the other. It is our sin that supplies the strength for the satanic strongholds over our cities.

The church's greatest need is not to declare war on hell but to declare war on our own sin and disunity. If we don't clean up our act and establish a biblical foundation and some accountability in spiritual warfare, foolishness is going to derail the prayer movement.

The American church must move into maturity. We are living in a day when we are to be displaying the mysteries of God to Satan and his rulers (see Eph. 3:10). But we are quickly losing our integrity.

Ten years ago there was a "fad" in evangelical prayer circles

that suggested no one could pray effectively unless he covered his head with a *tallith*, or Hebrew prayer shawl. It was the only way to pray.

Then we got hung up on the *shofar*. Blowing the ram's horn somehow legitimized warfare prayer. Surely, many thought, it must strike terror into the heart of Satan!

Spiritual "birthing" and "midwifery" followed that. Today warfare prayer is often accompanied by the waving of ceremonial swords. This is now the "official" way to pray.

We must return to the simplicity of asking and receiving. There is nothing wrong with our shows, shawls, *shofars* and swords. But they do not bother the enemy. God wants us to know that He legitimizes us. He is to be our focus. He alone holds the power that overcomes the evil one.

THE BATTLE STRATEGY

So what is our battle plan? We have to look at the way Jesus dealt with the enemy. In His life on earth He confronted Satan in the wilderness and demons in the streets, but He never intentionally confronted hell's princes directly. He never stormed the gates of hell.

Of course, He could have done it in a heartbeat, if it had been the will of God. But God had—and still has—another plan. He's going to let His bride do it! For Satan, it will be both a defeat and a humiliation.

But such an awesome assault will demand a well-devised strategy. This strategy will be built around the following four requirements for successful spiritual warfare:

1. Discipline. Eddie admits that his early childhood memories are becoming harder to access with each passing year. But one that has remained clear is a picture of his playing Pick-Up Sticks with his two younger brothers. The game is played with a handful of slender wooden sticks, which, when dropped from their can, form a pile on the floor.

Each player tries to remove one stick at a time without moving another stick. If the player moves a stick other than the one he is attempting to pull out of the pile, his turn ends. If he doesn't, he keeps the stick he removes. The one who collects the most sticks wins.

Winning requires strategic thinking and a steady hand to pull out the right stick, in the right order, at just the right time.

Eddie's youngest brother would grow impatient with the tedious process and would carelessly thrust in his hand to grab a stick. At his young age, he didn't have the discipline needed to win. If the church is going to succeed at spiritual warfare, we must become disciplined soldiers.

2. Spiritual mapping. A company called Controlled Demolition Incorporated (CDI) is the premier imploder of large buildings. The Leauzeaux family of Baltimore owns this business, which specializes in converting skyscrapers on crowded downtown streets into a pile of dust in what appears to be only seconds.

Jack Leauzeaux, the family's patriarch and the son of a missionary, says that they actually spend months on each project, studying how the building they've been hired to remove has been built. They test its material and learn its strengths and weaknesses. They pre-weaken strategic supports within the structure.

Then, using blueprints, they

skillfully place explosive charges throughout the building that are all wired to the same control console. The charges are timed to go off in proper sequence to cause the building to implode, not explode. It literally collapses upon itself.

On "D-day" the Leauzeauxes clear the area and press one button. Suddenly and rather spectacularly, a multi-story building is reduced to rubble that can be trucked off to a landfill! Jack Leauzeaux says, "Our goal is to produce maximum results with the smallest amount of explosive."

That's what we want to do in the church, also. So we use spiritual mapping to discover how Satan has achieved his advantage in our cities and nations. Through diligent, time-consuming study, dedicated warriors learn both the strengths and weaknesses of his spiritual structures in preparation for an attack.

3. Discretion. The Leauzeaux family carefully plan their demolitions. They would never opt to randomly throw sticks of dynamite at a building they were planning to bring down.

Why? Because there would be too great a risk of collateral damage. We must likewise be discreet in laying out our battle plans.

4. Discernment. Along with spiritual mapping, discernment gives us direction in spiritual warfare. We must learn to hear the voice of God if we expect to get orders from headquarters. One way we do this is through prophetic intercession.

In America's Desert Storm war against Iraq, the world was introduced to an infrared technology called "night vision." This technology enables pilots and soldiers to see targets shrouded in pitch darkness as though they were sitting in the full light of day. America's

planes and tanks and even its infantry were equipped with these lenses.

Prophetic intercession is the spiritual warfare equivalent of "night vision" goggles. It enables the intercessor to locate specific, strategic, satanic targets against which to pray.

Through revelatory gifts of words of knowledge, discerning of spirits, wisdom, and spiritual sight and hearing, God shows His warriors the strengths and weaknesses of enemy strongholds. He also reveals to them how and when they are to take action.

We are always to be Spirit-led, not need-driven. This is particularly important if we are going to embrace the Father's battle plan and timetable and move only at His command. We must resist the impulse to get ahead of Him.

During the Desert Storm war, the entire world held its breath waiting for the U.S.-led allied ground forces to assault Iraqi military positions. It seemed to many of us that the ground war would never begin. But we were told that the ground war could not begin until the air war was completed.

When the air missions had been accomplished, the ground war began as promised. And, as hoped, the ground war was a piece of cake. The strength of Saddam Hussein's troops had been dissipated. His foot soldiers were disillusioned, tired and hungry, and their communications system was devastated. They surrendered on the spot!

In the spiritual war against the forces of darkness we see just the opposite. The ground war must come first. Yet prophetic intercessors can almost taste the air war. Warfare-prayer intercessors are revving up their engines and can hardly wait until the Lord releases them against the gates of hell.

Some are wondering, *Why*

hot now? Others, out of impatience and presumption, decide to call their own shots. Like spiritual Rambos they move out, often without directives from our commander, Jesus Christ. The result is that they conduct spiritual sorties (air raids) with only minimal success—and little change in their churches and cities.

SATAN'S KINGDOM IS REAL

Satan has staked out a territory and populated it with all kinds of evil beings—from run-of-the-mill demons that seek to harass and corrupt lives to the powerful princes and rulers that Paul writes about in Ephesians 6:12.

Satan desires to dominate world affairs and to prevent the lost from hearing the gospel. So far, his tactics have been effective. Although the church has had 2,000 years to dismantle the kingdom of darkness, we have not succeeded.

Consequently, the majority of people on this planet have yet to hear the name of Jesus. Satan has "blinded the minds of them which believe not, lest the light of the glorious gospel of Christ, who is the image of God, should shine unto them" (2 Cor. 4:3-4, KJV).

He is understandably proud of this fact. He boasts: " 'By the strength of my hand I have done it, and by my wisdom, for I am prudent; also I have removed the boundaries of the people, and have robbed their treasuries; so I have put down the inhabitants like a valiant man. My hand has found like a nest the riches of the people, and as one gathers eggs that are left, I have gathered all the earth; and there was no one who moved his wing, nor opened his mouth with even a peep' " (Is. 10:13-14, NKJV).

Thankfully, God is doing a new thing in our day. The Spirit of the Lord is brooding over the church, and for the first time in history, prayer for the nations is going forth from every continent (see Ps. 2:8). The church is taking the completion of the Great Commission seriously.

Best of all, the Father is answering our prayers. A massive spiritual harvest is now occurring around the world! Every day three times as many people are being saved as were being saved on an average day just 10 years ago.

We believe that we are the generation who will see the church, Christ's mature bride. Stand in unity and declare to those ancient evil princes, "No more!"

After all, Jesus promised that the gates of hell would not prevail against the church (see Matt. 16:18). We will see the fulfillment of His promise if we refrain from storming these gates until He tells us how and when to do it.

—Alice and Eddie Smith are cofounders and officers of the U.S. Prayer Center in Houston, Texas. They are both members of America's National Prayer Committee, the International Strategic Prayer Network and the International Reconciliation Coalition. Alice conducts seminars, retreats and conferences on a variety of subjects including intercessory prayer, spiritual intimacy, personal freedom, spiritual warfare and spiritual mapping. Eddie is a contributor to several magazines, as well as an occasional guest on CBN's 700 Club.

Reprinted by permission Charisma Magazine and Strang Communications Company.

December 1999, Charisma

LESSON 9

WHY WOULD GOD ALLOW EVIL?

MAIN PRINCIPLE

God gets blamed for everything! Do we blame God for the problems in our lives? Do we turn to God only when there is a problem? God doesn't create evil, but He does use it to cause us to grow more in His likeness.

THE DEVIL, DEMONS & SPIRITUAL WARFARE

compiled by John Archer

A PANEL OF EXPERTS ANSWER 10 OFTEN-ASKED QUESTIONS ABOUT THE CHURCH'S BATTLE AGAINST THE FORCES OF DARKNESS.

The Scriptures tell us that the church is at war with personal, supernatural evil. Demonic beings led by Satan battle against the kingdom of God, blinding the minds of the lost, instigating evil and inflicting suffering.

But their work is not going unchallenged.

On February 12, 1990, a select group of intercessors convened in Southern California to discuss the role of prayer in overcoming territorial spirits and winning the lost. Their insights on the subject of spiritual warfare were not derived solely through Bible study, but also through personal experiences in challenging the forces of darkness.

The group—which included C. Peter Wagner, John Dawson, Cindy Jacobs, Jack Hayford, Larry Lea, Gwen Shaw, Dick Bernal, Tom White, Joy Dawson and Dick Eastman—eventually became known as the Spiritual Warfare Network. This network has since become an important part of the United Prayer Track of the A.D. 2000 Movement, a cooperative effort mobilizing

Christians to evangelize the unreached by the year 2000.

On February 21-23, 1994, the Spiritual Warfare Network is sponsoring a landmark national conference in Anaheim, California. Open to ministers and lay leaders, this gathering will feature interaction with the foremost experts in the spiritual warfare movement.

As a prelude to the conference, *Charisma* asked several of those experts to tackle some tough questions about the devil, demons and spiritual warfare. We have published their answers both to inform and to provoke more discussion on this often controversial topic.

Q: Can Satan or evil spirits read our thoughts?

C. Peter Wagner: We must avoid the common error of imagining that Satan has some of God's attributes. Only God is omniscient. He knows everything, including what is in our minds. Satan does not have this ability.

The fact that Christians must confront demons *audibly* to secure someone's deliverance is strong evidence that they cannot read our minds. Nevertheless, dwelling on carnal thoughts such as persistent sexual fantasies separates us from God and opens us to demonic influences.

Francis Frangipane: The devil can infiltrate our thoughts with his own. But he cannot read a mind that is "renewed in knowledge according to the image of [God]" (Col. 3:10; see also Eph. 4:23).

Let me qualify that statement. The demonic view of our world is from the inside out, rather than the outside in—demons see a person's spirit first and then the flesh. The glory the disciples saw on the Mount of Transfiguration was what demons always saw when they looked at Jesus. Demons recognized Him as the Son of God because they saw the fullness of God's glory in His life.

So I believe Satan can discern our general thought patterns

by the brightness of our countenance. He knows if we are earnestly yielded to the Holy Spirit.

But the devil cannot understand the specifics of our prayers, our meditations or our worship when we are surrendered to God. Only when we are in rebellion against God can the devil barricade himself inside our minds, where he has access to our thoughts.

Even if Satan could read our minds, he couldn't grasp spiritual truths or motives. Although the devil overheard Jesus say He was to die and be raised the third day, he did not comprehend God's strategy, nor did he realize Christ's crucifixion would be his undoing.

Tom White: Evil beings may indeed project thoughts into the mind, moods into the emotions and impulses into the will from their external vantage point. But the enemy cannot read our thoughts if we are free from internal demonization.

I believe a mind set on what the Spirit desires is a sanctuary impenetrable by evil spirits (see Rom. 8:5). This has been proven to me in deliverance sessions, because demons don't know the strategy that I'm considering to expel them.

Let's recognize, however, that these beings have been deceiving and afflicting people since creation —so they are adept at predicting behavior. By reading facial expressions, voice intonations, and behavioral nuances, they can often predict what we will do. But this does not mean they have access to our thoughts.

Q: How can I tell the difference between the voice of the Holy Spirit and the voice of an evil spirit?

John Dawson: There is an unmistakable quality to the good Shepherd's voice that cannot be duplicated either by our imagination or by any evil spirit. Jesus said, "My sheep hear My voice, and I know them, and they follow Me" (John 10:27).

The key is to seek God until you know Him. The greatest protection against deception by the enemy is familiarity with the Master's voice found through spending time in His presence.

Francis Frangipane: When seeking the Lord's direction, remember that the Holy Spirit seeks to glorify God in Christ. Accordingly, what the Holy Spirit says will be aimed at exalting God through our decision.

But the devil seeks to glorify self within us; he savors the things that are of man and not God. So when we seek the Lord, we should ask ourselves: Who will be glorified by our decision —God or us?

When an inner voice or impression illuminates sin in your life, remember that the Holy Spirit convicts; He does not condemn. When the Holy Spirit convicts us of sin, He is clear and precise, offering not only exposure, but hope of forgiveness. But an evil spirit speaks with condemnation, offering us no way out of our wickedness.

Tom White: God will never speak anything contrary to His revealed Word or character. I've found that the Holy Spirit is gentle, clear and consistent in His leading. He leads by an inward prompting that has a "ring of rightness" to it.

Often other people or circumstances will confirm the Spirit's voice. If we are truly submitted to Him, we will be open to other's scrutiny and correction. The Father's promptings will always result in redemptive purpose and good fruit.

The devil, on the other hand, is sly, often bringing doubts concerning the reliability of God's character. Devilish promptings always lead to unfruitful ends.

Often, we can only tell through time whether we have followed the Spirit's voice, the enemy's voice or our own carnal thoughts. Our protection is abidance in the Word and accountability to godly leadership in a local church.

Q: How can I tell the difference between a human impulse and a demonic temptation?

Tom White: Many Christians wrestle with persistent, compulsive problems such as anger, lust and bitterness. They are overtaken by some thing that seems to compel behavior.

But let's not be too quick to call this demonic. In Romans 7 the apostle Paul described sin as a sort of compulsive force. In many cases involving persistent sin, the influences of the world, the flesh and the devil do overlap. Trying to determine the exact source is difficult and often pointless.

In dealing with sin, believers should practice two disciplines: First, we must readily confess our sin, reckon ourselves dead to its power and receive the Lord's forgiveness. Second, we should tell the accuser to depart because "there is no condemnation to those who are in Christ Jesus." The fruits of peace and fresh joy should follow.

If there is no peace or victory through treating this problem as carnality, pray with a discerning Christian to check for oppression. If you sense that demonic forces are manipulating you, actively and immediately resist them in the authority of Jesus' name and blood. Enlist the power of the Spirit and the holy angels to drive away the darkness.

Do this privately, or with a prayer partner or group. If it is the

February 1994, Charisma

devil, and you are also dealing with your sin, the Lord will drive him off. If it isn't demonic, I believe the Lord will lead you to the root of the problem.

Q: What are some typical ways in which people can come under demonic bondage?

Tom White: Through numerous encounters, I have identified four major sources of oppression:

- The personal, persistent practice of moral compromise -- either as unbelievers or believers -- can open doors to the influence of evil spirits. Occultic practices, idolatry of any kind, bitterness, hate, persistent sexual sin or fleshly indulgence are just some of the sins that invite demonic bondage.

- Demonic oppression can come through the victimizing sins of others, such as rape, incest or exposure to occultic ritual.

- The sins of others in one's family history can open doors to evil spirits, which then try to invade subsequent generations.

- Ministry activity that draws the enemy's attention can be another avenue for demonic oppression. For example, launching a prayer initiative in your community or sponsoring a youth outreach may signal the enemy of your seriousness to penetrate his perimeter of deception. Any serious threat to the domain of darkness may draw "return fire." The wise servant will engage in "pre-emptive prayer strikes" to minimize these attacks.

Esther Ilnisky: Satan's strategies are as cleverly placed and well-

camouflaged as a mine field. If we lack discernment or fail to respond appropriately, we could fall into his traps. Here are some things that invite demonic bondage:

- *Self-initiated vulnerability.* Treating the devil and demons as a laughing matter is dangerous. A smug, nonchalant attitude toward evil spirits is an open invitation to demonic bondage.
- *Flirting with the satanic.* Don't consider yourself immune to the satanic influences found in seemingly innocent entertainment. Have nothing to do with reading materials, movies, music, games or hobbies that have occultic themes or practices.
- *Dabbling.* Curiosity and experimentation are open pits. Stay away from yoga, séances, magic, spells, hexes, Ouija boards, horoscopes and other occultic activities.
- *Wrong company.* Socializing with people who participate in occultic practices is like knowingly exposing yourself to a contagious disease.
- *Ambivalence.* Double-minded people are unstable in all their ways. Don't bargain with the devil or compromise with evil.
- *Rebellion against divine order.* Remember: "Rebellion is as the sin of witchcraft" (1 Sam. 15:23). People who are not properly submitted to spiritual authority, or who murmur against their spiritual leaders, jerk themselves out from under God's protective care.

C. Peter Wagner: The enemy's most common entrance into someone's life is through continuous, unrepentant sin. The sin of unforgiveness may be most potent. But if we daily live with a pure heart, we will draw near to God and resist Satan, just as James 4:7 says.

Satan, however, seeks to devour even believers living in holiness, and at times his blows are successful. He can use trauma as an entry point. He can also use curses launched at believers by individuals or groups. Fortunately, we have weapons to prevent this from happening and for healing when it does.

Q: How can you distinguish between a psychiatric disorder and demonization?

Tom White: I have prayed with a number of people suffering from schizophrenia, manic depression, multiple personality disorder and psychotic episodes. In some cases, demons attach to and aggravate the condition. In others, there is clear psychiatric malfunction.

With such disorders, there are symptoms of internal voices, extreme paranoia, religious delusions and uncontrolled behaviors. Psychiatrist Kurt Koch, author of *Occult Bondage and Deliverance,* made the valuable observation that the mentally ill person is quick to talk about voices and spirits, whereas the demonized individual is typically not —evil spirits want to stay hidden.

I have learned to distinguish psychiatric disorders from demonization through careful observation —disorders fit predictable patterns with observable symptoms —and through testing at two levels.

First, I seek to interact with a person over certain truths concerning Jesus Christ or God's Word. I may ask him to read a portion of Scripture. Often I will open an interview with prayer. I watch for clear negative reaction to authority and the working of the Holy Spirit.

On a second level, if the person is agreeable, I will do a direct test: With eyes open, relying on the Holy Spirit, I will command any

February 1994, Charisma

enemies of Christ present to manifest themselves.

Still, it is important to realize that a mentally disturbed person can easily create a demon if you ask for one. Accurate discernment is necessary to distinguish a demon from a disorder.

Esther Ilnisky: Usually a person with a mental disorder will respond positively to psychiatric treatment, medication, counseling and prayer. But a demonized person will not show long-term improvement from any of these means.

Moreover, a demonized person frequently exhibits unexpected physical reactions—at times violent. This can produce some frighteningly bizarre symptoms.

- personality changes or the exhibition of multiple personalities
- mocking, jeering
- profuse use of obscenities
- preoccupation with sexually perverse, violent or demonic practices

However, a demonized person can say the right words and behave impeccably. So the gift of "discerning of spirits" is crucial for Christian counselors.

Q: Are there specific days or seasons when evil forces are stronger?

Esther Ilnisky: Definitely. I believe that any Christian holiday alerts all the echelons of darkness to mobilize their forces for attack. A holiday like Halloween that promotes Satanism and the occult leaves a wide-open atmosphere for demons to operate. Also, all false, anti-Christ celebrations of "religious" holidays release demonic activity worldwide.

Tom White: Times of heightened evil activity often coincide with ce-

lestial changes, such as new and full moons, the summer and winter solstices and the fall and spring equinoxes. Such observances trace back to ancient pagan practices related to the worship of astral deities.

In formal satanism, there are documented unholy days when certain rituals and sacrifices (animal and human) are performed: February 2, March 20 (spring equinox), April 26- May 1, June 21 (summer solstice), August 3, September 22 (fall equinox), October 29-November 1 (All Hallow's Eve) and December 22-24 (winter solstice).

These seasons should be opportunities for the church to enter into strong praise, worship and celebration of the lordship of Christ.

Q: If the archangel Michael didn't dare to rebuke the devil (Jude 9), shouldn't we refrain from addressing Satan?

Francis Frangipane: The scriptural platform the church stands on concerning spiritual warfare against principalities and powers can be found in several passages (see Luke 10:19, Eph. 6:12). In light of these and other verses, it's interesting that such a stir has been made over Jude's passing reference to Michael and the devil.

Jude's purpose was not to offer direct, theological insight into doctrines of spiritual warfare, but to identify and expose false Christians who had crept into the church. One means of identifying them was their blatant reviling of angelic majesties, which are holy, not fallen, angels. The context surrounding Jude 9 is a comparison between these corrupt individuals who reviled angels and Michael who refused to revile even the devil.

From the text we can conclude that it is procedurally wrong

to revile the devil. We should never mock Satan nor brag about what we are going to do to him. Yet, I believe we slip into error when we read more into Jude 9 than is there.

Jude 9 says Michael did not bring a "railing judgment" against the devil. There is a large difference between a "railing judgment" and what God's Word calls "the judgment written" (Ps. 149:9). Psalm 149 tells us that participating with God in decisive judgment is an honor for His "godly ones."

Speaking to principalities is not a railing judgment, but an act of strategic obedience to the written will of God. Apart from Christ, the church has no credentials to speak against Satan. But Christ in us raises the position of the church "far above principalities and powers."

Having been born both of the flesh and the Spirit, the church is a hybrid. The heavenly places are our domain, not Satan's. But our assault against the enemy comes from God's initiative, not our own. To exercise Christ's authority, we must live in His nature. We cannot just be angry against the devil and rail against him with fleshly judgments. We must know the judgment written, as well as God's primary purposes in warfare and His overall strategy with the church. Someone greater than Michael dwells within the church; it must be Christ who confronts the devil through us.

Q: Can evil spirits inhabit inanimate objects? If so, how does this occur?

C. Peter Wagner: Evil spirits may attach themselves to inanimate objects used in occult practices or pagan worship. Any discerning Christian who has spent time in an animistic culture has no question about this.

February 1994, Charisma

Deuteronomy 32:17 and 1 Corinthians 10:19-20, for instance, clearly associate idols with demons. This is why idolatry is so categorically condemned in the Bible.

Idols are nothing. Pieces of wood or stone are no threat to the kingdom of God. The real threats are the demonic personalities that have attached themselves to idols, most frequently at the invitation of humans.

Q: What evidence is there that evil spirits control geographical territories such as cities or countries?

Cindy Jacobs: Ephesians 6:12 speaks of the believer's warfare "against principalities against powers, against the rulers of the darkness of this age, against spiritual hosts of wickedness in the heavenly places." Bible scholars agree that this verse suggests a hierarchy of demonic powers.

Daniel 10, which describes celestial warfare between God's angels and the "princes" of Persia and Greece (vv. 13, 20), gives further insight into the nature of this hierarchy. Based on this passage, demonic agents are apparently assigned to the sponsorship and control of territories and communities.

I believe certain demonic forces mass to different regions to fortify particular types of evil. Certain cities may be strongholds of idolatry, sensual sin or certain kinds of religious spirits.

The ancient city Pergamos could be considered a territorial stronghold. In Revelation 2:13, the city is described as "where Satan's throne is." According to *Unger's Bible Dictionary:* "The city was greatly addicted to idolatry, and its grove... was filled with statues and altars."

My experience has confirmed these biblical passages. In September 1990 Generals of Intercession met with local intercessors in the city of Mar del Plata, Argentina.

The intercessors discerned four major territorial spirits ruling over Mar del Plata and a "strong man" ruler who reigned over the four. After a time of fasting, repentance and prayer, 300 people began praying against the ruling spirit of witchcraft.

We discovered later that one of the witches who had been invoking curses against the city's pastors dropped dead -- at the same moment we began praying. Although saddened about the death, we recognized that God was pulling down the city's demonic strongholds.

Q: What are the keys to accomplishing spiritual breakthrough in a city or region?

Bob Beckett: A key element in the deliverance of an individual's personality is to determine the sins, wounds and offenses that have opened him up to dark influences. It's the same with a city's personality.

Hebrews 11:10 describes Abraham as looking for "a city which has foundations, whose builder and maker is God." The word *foundation*, according to *Thayer's Greek Lexicon,* "is used metaphorically for the beginning principles of truth and belief systems." Thus Abraham was looking for a city where God Himself could be established in the city's belief system or personality.

In 1 Corinthians 3:10-12, the apostle Paul uses the same word *foundation* in reference to the human personality. So the key to a city's personality is its foundation! Abraham was not looking for a perfect city but rather a city that he could inject his beliefs and principles into, thus changing that city.

In Matthew 11:22-23, Jesus' lament over Capernaum suggests the city has a corporate personality. Jesus tells Capernaum to be careful, or she will be judged for her actions and her belief system—her personality.

Of course this does not mean that a city has a living soul. But it does indicate that a city's belief system controls its actions and future. Every city has a distinct personality that was formed by the beliefs and experiences of its founding citizens.

By studying the foundations of a city, we can form a spiritual picture of its true personality. I like the way Peter Wagner puts it: "Learn to see the city not as it appears, but as it really is."

John Dawson: Cities can be transformed! The early days of the Salvation Army demonstrate the gospel's power to radically change the life of a city. Founder General Booth clearly identified satanic bondages of alcoholism, prostitution and injustice in certain cities. His "army" penetrated the city with the gospel, employing citywide strategies to bring citywide victories.

Discerning the nature of the enemy's lies is half the battle. Whole countries are kept in darkness by satanic lies that have become cornerstones of a particular culture. But this stark darkness is not impenetrable. Scripture says that one day Christians will look upon Satan in amazement saying, "Is this the one who made the nations tremble?" (Is. 14:16). He will be seen for who he really is -- small and impotent, having held nations captive only through the stubborn will of people who embrace his lies.

Thus Christians contribute to a city's victory when they identify the spiritual opposition and its manifestations. Here is a list of four areas of research to aid the intercessor:

- Look at your city's secular history. Why is this city here and what moral and spiritual trends were involved in its founding?

- Look at your city's Christian history. Research the life of God's people in it, particularly during times of revival. Discover what God has revealed to our forefathers of faith.

- Distinguish what the present-day intercessors, spiritual fathers and those with prophetic insight in your city are saying.

- Study your city's demographics. Where do people live? How may are in poverty, and why are they in poverty? What are the trends? Get the facts. Spiritual warfare does not operate in a vacuum.

Once you have discerned the opposition, begin warfare with worship, wait on the Lord for revelation about His strategy, and then travail in prayer until you see God's purposes. It is important to humbly identify with the sins of the city and to call on God for mercy. If you are tempted to greed and stinginess, counter it with exorbitant generosity. Overcome pride with humility, lust with purity, fear with faith.

Pray with faith. The size of your faith is revealed by your plans and expectations.

Envision this: You let God's heart for the city become your heart. You and your friends begin a citywide prayer movement. Local churches find revival, followed by an awakening among non-Christians, reformation of the society and a new expression of world mission.

God waits for a people who will see Him as He is, then follow Him to victory.

Francis Frangipane: Jesus Himself taught that a house divided cannot stand. As far as turning our cities toward God, our posture against the enemy is only as strong as our stand with one another. Thus, full-scale confrontation against principalities and powers should not be launched without certain preparations within the citywide church.

The bulk of this preparation is not sophisticated spiritual warfare, rather basics such as repentance and reconciliation between churches and ethnic groups.

God did not anoint the "deliverer" to drive away Israel's foes until *after* Israel had repented toward God. We do not have an unlimited range of authority against principalities if the people within those strongholds are unrepentant. Repentance must precede deliverance.

The "sword of the Spirit" raised against the enemy is the Word of God. One edge of God's sword is Scripture. The other edge is the living Word of God: what the Spirit is saying *now* to the church. God's Word is the beginning and end of our communication with the devil on whatever scale we confront him.

—John Archer was the editorial director for Charisma magazine.

Reprinted by permission Charisma Magazine and Strang Communications Company.

February 1994, Charisma

INCENSE AND THUNDER

By Dudley Hall

PRAYING IN THE SPIRIT WILL OVERCOME YOUR WEAKNESSES AND BREATHE NEW LIFE INTO YOUR MINISTRY.

Likewise the Spirit also helps in our weaknesses. For we do not know what we should pray for as we ought, but the Spirit Himself makes intercession for us with groanings which cannot be uttered. Now He who searches the hearts knows what the mind of the Spirit is, because He makes intercession for the saints according to the will of God" (Rom. 8:26-27, NKJV).

I had been away from my family for several days on a ministry trip. Each night I looked forward to the phone call home to find out how my wife, son and daughter were doing. The calls were always filled with joy as my wife and each of my kids told me the details of their day. After a tiring day of work, I always looked forward to the refreshment that came from those calls home.

But one of those routine phone calls changed my life. It occurred on a Wednesday night. I was scheduled to return home early the next morning. When my wife, Betsy, picked up the phone, I could tell something was wrong. She began to tell me about the severe pain she was having in her arm. It was so severe she couldn't sleep. She had bright red stripes up and down her arm.

From her training as a nurse, Betsy knew something was severely wrong. Meekly she said: "It only started this morning. Now it's all over my whole arm and even my shoulder. I think it might be staph infection."

Then she related how earlier that day she'd taken our daughter, Karis, to the doctor to have a routine checkup. The doctor reported that he thought she might be a candidate for juvenile diabetes. But that wasn't all. Our son, David, had swallowed a tack earlier in the day and already had been taken to the emergency room.

I wanted to gather all of my family into my arms, but I was 1,000 miles away. It was late at night; there was no way I could get there until the next day. All I could do was pray.

That night as I knelt beside a bed in a dreary motel room, I found that my burden was greater than my ability to express. All I could do was groan. Every once in a while I could make out some intelligible words such as, "Oh, God!" or "Mercy." But putting together an intelligible, rational prayer was beyond my ability. I really don't know how long this prayer session went on. It seemed like an eternity, but finally there was an answer that floated to my consciousness: "Your wife will be fine in a few days. Your daughter's illness is an opportunity for you and your wife to learn faith. Your son is in no danger."

I can't explain how I knew that those words were from my heavenly Father. I can only testify that I knew. I also knew that I had experienced an encounter with God in prayer that was different from anything I'd had before. God had come to me and helped me pray a prayer that He was now answering. I was learning that God is so interested in our prayer life, He not only starts our prayer life and ends it, He also helps us pray.

We don't know what we ought to pray for, but the Spirit Himself intercedes for us with groans that words cannot express.

WEAKNESS IS NO OBSTACLE

The first thing we learn about Holy Spirit-assisted prayer is that our weaknesses don't disqualify us from participating in eternal purposes. Prayer is our part. It is our privilege and responsibility apart from God's intervening and helping us. It is His mercy from first to last.

Romans 8 is one of the most beautiful passages of Scripture in all the Bible because it describes the life given to us through faith in Jesus Christ. This life was imparted to us by the presence of the Holy Spirit, who has united with our spirits. Through this passage, several important functions of the Holy Spirit come to light.

1. He gives life to our bodies. The Holy Spirit came to give life to our mortal bodies. Those bodies, which were dead because of sin, are granted the ability to have the very life of Jesus in them. We're not just the chemical components of a fleshly body; actually we're clay vessels inhabited by the very presence of God.

2. He fosters intimate relationship with God. The Holy Spirit came into us to make our relationship with God an intimate one. We did not receive a spirit that makes us slaves again to fear, but we received the Spirit of sonship, and by Him we cry, "Abba, Father."

It is the Holy Spirit's revelation to our inner man that God is no longer just the creator of the universe and the judge of all mankind, but He is the heavenly Father to those who came to Him by faith in Christ Jesus. This is no longer just a cognitive knowledge but now a real experience for those who enjoy the ministry of the Holy Spirit in their hearts.

3. He testifies that we are children of God. The Spirit Himself testifies with our spirits that we are God's children. We are no longer left to simple, rational propositions to believe that we are the children of God. We can discern from an inner knowing that we are His children and are safe in His hands. Apart from the ministry of the Holy Spirit, this knowledge is left to our memories or rational deductions.

> "THE FIRST THING WE LEARN ABOUT HOLY SPIRIT-ASSISTED PRAYER IS THAT OUR WEAKNESSES DONT DISQUALIFY US FROM PARTICIPATING IN ETERNAL PURPOSES"

4. He helps us in our weakness. "Likewise the Spirit helps us in our weakness" (Rom. 8:26). This phrase comes in the context of a passage in which Paul discusses the groaning of creation as it awaits its final redemption. He describes the conflict that we have as human beings who are part of a fallen creation, yet are indwelt by eternal life.

While creation groans, waiting for the children of God to be revealed and for the culmination of the kingdom of God, we as believers experience something of the limitation of human beings. Yet this conflict of our limitations does not prohibit us from participating in God's eternal plan for us.

God created us to rule on the earth with Him through our prayers. It is such an incredible thought that God allows us feeble human beings to participate in His eternal purposes and that He comes to assist us in knowing how to pray.

TIMES OF GROANING

All who have taken prayer seriously have experienced those times of groaning. We know we should pray, we even want to pray, but we don't know how to pray. We may have concerns for our own families, for instance. We don't know whether to pray that our children never have trouble or to pray that they'll have trouble so they'll discover the grace of God.

Regarding our finances, do we pray for more resources, or do we pray that God will give us a contentment with what we already have? As we pray for our nation, do we pray for prosperity, or do we pray that the nation experience more crises so we'll repent and return to the God who is the source of all our blessing? These and a thousand other issues can become a point of consternation for us when we have taken seriously the mandate from our creator to manage this earth through prayer.

The good news of this passage is that through my groans and the assistance of the Holy Spirit, I can pray beyond my understanding. If my prayers are answered based on my intelligence, or even my purist motives, I can be assured that many, if not most, prayers would go unanswered. This passage gives me hope that when I've come to the end of myself and don't even know how to express my prayer, the Holy Spirit will come to my aid and assist me by praying both for me and through me.

Maybe we should point out that the experience of groaning can be offensive. None of us likes to be in a position where we are out of control. But when the burden is so deep that we can't express it fully, we are in a place beyond our understanding. I don't know about you, but when I pray I've found that my head fights to get ahead of my heart. And all the while God seeks to build up my inner man so that I am ruled more by my spirit than just my thoughts. (See 1 Cor. 2:11-12; Eph. 3:14-16.)

Groaning is not a very sophisticated way to pray. It doesn't give much solace to our pride and independent self-esteem. Many times we seek to avoid situations that make us desperate, but it has been accurately said, "It is only when the desperation factor exceeds our embarrassment factor that we are open to a new work from God."

PRAYING IN TONGUES

I'm sure the question arises, Does this passage in Romans 8 speak of praying in tongues? There has been disagreement among scholars about this. It seems to me that this passage would include the ability to pray in tongues, but it doesn't describe that experience exclusively.

We can pray in the Spirit whether we are using the gift of tongues or not. Just as we live in the Spirit and walk in the Spirit, we can pray in the Spirit, which essentially means to pray with a consciousness that the Holy Spirit is motivating our prayer, guiding our prayer and answering our prayer. It is an attitude of total dependence upon God to align our will with His will, which helps us express the burdens of our hearts and receive the blessings that He intended.

It's unfortunate that praying in tongues has become controversial in the body of Christ and has caused many to retreat from the privilege of praying in the Spirit. We don't have to be afraid of anything God gives. The ability to pray in tongues is a gift from God that allows us to communicate with God, Spirit-to-spirit, without the full use of understanding (see 1 Cor. 14:2).

Because tongues is a gift, it's something we must receive when we desire it, ask for it and believe it. Obviously, if we don't want it, God doesn't force that gift upon us. The benefit of the gift is that it edifies the believer (see 1 Cor. 14:4).

Some have concluded that it is wrong to want to edify self, but I don't believe Paul was referring to the egocentric self. Rather, he was talking about one's whole being. It isn't wrong to want to be edified -- that is, to be energized and built up in the Spirit. We study the Scriptures for that purpose. We pray and meditate for that purpose. We fast and practice solitude and silence for that purpose. We listen to tapes and attend conferences --all so our spirits can be edified.

Desire for edification is not self-centered. It is what we do as a result of our edification that determines whether or not our motives are pure. If we try to use any gift that we have from God as a trophy to prove our spirituality, then we've moved from servanthood to idolatry. If we use it as a toy to play with, we are revealing our immaturity. If we use it as a tool that God has given us to subdue the earth in partnership with Him, then we have properly found the use of His gift.

As we said earlier, this passage in Romans probably isn't referring directly to the gift of tongues when it speaks of the Holy Spirit coming and helping us in our weakness. The implication here is not that He prays in our stead but that He helps us to pray. He takes what is inexpressible in our minds and turns it into a viable prayer. We mustn't lose the glory of this blessing in all the questions we may have about how it works. The bottom line is that God has graced us with the person of the Holy Spirit to give us life, to guide us in life, and even to help us pray when the prayers we need go beyond our human limitations. We can pray beyond our understanding by relying on the Holy Spirit.

FRUITS OF SPIRIT-ASSISTED PRAYER

Spirit-assisted prayer, in its end, is fruitful. First, the Holy Spirit always prays according to the will of God because He is God Himself. The Holy Spirit prays according to the sovereign purposes of God. If we want to know what He's praying, we can again become acquainted with those sovereign purposes. He is able to take the mystery of the burdens of our hearts, mix it with the sovereign purposes of God, and come out with a prayer that pleases the Father and gets an answer.

This type of prayer also releases burdens. Many people go through life totally burdened down, not understanding that many of those burdens are God's call upon them for involvement in His eternal purposes. When we yield to Holy Spirit-assisted praying, we find burdens lifted from us that could never be taken away by counseling, drugs or religious activity. They are there to bring us into total dependence on God, who desires desperately to bless us with His life.

Another fruit of Spirit-assisted praying is that it activates our faith. It requires faith to pray with a groan. We have to believe in the promises of God, that He actually is doing something in us in order for us to pray like this. In this type of praying, we not only can't figure out how God is going to answer it, we also can't figure out how to ask it.

September/October 1999, Ministries Today

This kind of prayer takes away all of our excuses. We no longer can say, "I don't pray because I don't know how." God, in effect, says, "I'll come and pray with you and for you." We also can't say, "Well, I'm too burdened to pray." The burden is the call to pray.

We can't say: "I'm afraid to pray. I'm afraid I'll pray with the wrong motives." God has said that He'll help us pray according to His will. With no excuses left, our only recourse is to accept our role as God has defined it—to pray: "Your kingdom come. Your will be done on earth as it is in heaven."

Father, thank You for being so intent on our participation with You in accomplishing eternal purposes. Thank You for the ministry of the Holy Spirit, who comes to our aid to help us pray beyond our capabilities. Thank You for the burdens that call us to prayer. And finally, thank You for answering the prayer You started in our hearts. Amen.

—Dudley Hall is the founder of Successful Christian Living Ministries and a recognized teacher intent on equipping the body of Christ. He is gifted in empowering men to embrace their masculine spirituality and leadership. His books include *Men in Their Own Skin* and *Grace Works, Incense & Thunder.*

HOW TO DONATE TO ZOE MINISTRIES

Help us deliver the message of Life throughout the World!

In addition to providing support for ZOE missions, curriculum development/translation and course scholarships, many of our translated materials will be donated to believers without resources to purchase them.

Would you prayerfully consider supporting this ministry?

YOU ARE ABLE TO MAKE A DONATION IN ANY OF THE FOLLOWING WAYS:

Online with PayPal Account or Credit Card via PayPal
This gives you a safe and easy way to make designated contributions.

Visit our website to make a secure online donation.
www.zoeministries.org/donor-partners/

By Automatic Bill Pay
Recurring donations to ZOE or to a designated ZOE missionary may be set up with your bank.

By Check
Please make checks payable to 'ZOE Ministries International'
Please don't write a missionary's name on the check. Instead include a separate note.
Our Address is – PO Box 2207, Arvada CO 80001-2207, USA

May God bless you richly for your support of this ministry!

"Now this is eternal life [zoe]: that they may know you, the only true God, and Jesus Christ, whom you have sent." - John 17:3

LESSON 10

DELIVER US FROM EVIL

MAIN PRINCIPLE

We see from our Lord's example that fasting does not change our position with God; it intensifies the power released toward satanic strongholds. Fasting should be a lifestyle!

GUIDELINES FOR FASTING
BODY, SOUL & SPIRIT

by Pamela Smith

The Bible is filled with examples of men and women of God who fasted and prayed: Moses, Elijah, Daniel, Ezra, Esther, Anna, Paul and, of course, Jesus. According to Luke, it was the Spirit of God who led Jesus into the wilderness to fast. Afterward, Jesus returned to Galilee "in the power of the Spirit" (Luke 4:14).

Martin Luther, John Calvin, Jonathan Edwards and Charles Finney were great men committed to fasting as an integral part of their spiritual lifestyles. Today, Campus Crusade for Christ founder Bill Bright, among others, is leading a call for Christians to fast and pray for nothing less than national and world revival.

For believers who recognize the power that is released through fasting and prayer, the question is not "*Should* I fast?" but "*How* should I fast?" As a nutritionist, I get equally as many questions about wise fasting as I do about wise eating. Here are the answers I give:

1. Purify your fast.

Fasting humbles us so we may receive more fully the grace and power of God, thus allowing us to walk more deeply in His purity and strength. It is a commitment to refrain from seeking physical food in order to seek God for spiritual food.

Enter into such a season out of obedience to God's call to fast and pray, "seek[ing] first His kingdom and His righteousness" (Matt. 6:33). Don't let the spiritual power that comes through fasting and prayer be stripped away by wrong motives such as a means to jump-start a weight-loss program or to "rid the body of poisons."

Research shows that going without food for prolonged periods not only causes your metabolism to slow drastically but actually produces many more toxins than regular eating. Fasting for selfish motives is, quite bluntly, starvation —with all of its detriments.

2. Prepare for your fast.

The day before your fast, eat smaller meals and snacks every 2-1/2 to three hours. To increase your body's store of energy, eat extra complex carbohydrates (bread, pasta or rice) at each of these meals, along with low-fat proteins (low-fat cheese, yogurt, turkey). Include a bedtime snack of cereal with milk or yogurt with fruit.

3. Consider your type of fast.

I recommend a "juice fast" for most busy people desiring to fast — not citrus juices (because of the citric acid), but "soft" juices like unsweetened apple, apple-cranberry or white grape. Drink 12 ounces of juice at your meal times and 6 ounces every two hours between meals, along with 2 to 3 quarts of water spread evenly throughout the day. Be careful with caffeine beverages, and avoid strenuous exercise.

Consider a "water fast" only if you are going into a "retreat" status and plan to withdraw totally from the physical demands of daily life. Drink lukewarm or cool water throughout the day and exercise moderately.

Some people, of course, should never fast, not even for 24 hours. These include women who are pregnant or breastfeeding; anyone diabetic or hypoglycemic; those with liver or kidney problems; and anyone who is malnourished. A better choice for such people is to sacrifice eating a particularly favorite food.

4. Pray with your fast.

Don't attempt to fast without the power hook-up of prayer. Many who fast try to carry on their normal, daily frenzy of activity only without food. God's grace is more than sufficient to meet our physical needs —even without eating —as long as we are feasting on His *spiritual* fare.

Jesus called those who hunger and thirst for righteousness "blessed," because they would be filled (Matt. 5:6). Hunger for God, and you will experience full-fillment.

5. Wisely break the fast.

Don't end your fast

with a huge meal or a feeding frenzy. Instead, eat a small snack of fruit and a low-fat protein. Eat another snack in two hours, then your first meal two hours later.

Your metabolism has greatly slowed in response to no food, and it will quickly store away large amounts eaten after the fast. That is why many find that pounds lost in fasting are often quickly regained.

When you heed God's call to fast, come before Him with a pure heart and follow sound nutritional guidelines. Make your fast meaningful-and wise.

—Pamela Smith is a nutritionist and energy coach, radio host, culinary consultant and author. Her books include *Food for Life, The Healthy Living Cookbook* and *The Smart Weigh.*

THE DEVIL'S DEADLINE!

by David Wilkerson

Woe to the inhabiters of the earth and of the sea! For the devil is come down unto you, having great wrath, because he knoweth that he hath but a short time (Revelation 12:12).

As followers of Jesus Christ, we are to be constantly aware that the devil is out to destroy us. Therefore, Paul says, we need to know as much as we can about the enemy's tactics and plans: "Lest Satan should get an advantage of us: for we are not ignorant of his devices" (2 Corinthians 2:11).

The above passage from Revelation tells us Satan has declared all-out war on God's saints. It also mentions that the devil has a deadline to complete his work: "...because he knoweth that he hath but a short time" (Revelation 12:12).

While many Christians slumber at this midnight hour, just as Jesus predicted, the devil is working ferociously, making preparation for war. He is keenly aware of the short time he has to accomplish his evil purposes —so he gives his eyes no rest. He is ever scheming, ever devising ways to harass and destroy the church of Jesus Christ!

So, when did the devil first realize his time was short? Did this knowledge come to him over the past century, as he read the signs of the times? Did he realize it as the nation of Israel was reborn, and nation began rising against nation? Did he recognize it when he saw a

great falling away from the Christian faith? Did he suddenly deduct from biblical references regarding these events that Jesus was about to return for his bride?

And when the devil came to this realization that his time was short, did he fly into a panic? Did he scramble to set up a "war room" on earth, planning a last-ditch, frantic battle against the church? Did he say to himself, "Time is slipping away. I've got to work fast, because I have only a short time before Christ returns!"

No! Satan's deadline was given to him centuries ago. It can be traced to "a great wonder" that took place in the heavens. This wonder was an incredible warfare, when Satan determined to destroy the Christ child:

"And there appeared a great wonder in heaven; a woman clothed with the sun, and the moon under her feet, and upon her head a crown of twelve stars: and she being with child cried, travailing in birth, and pained to be delivered" (verses 1-2).

The sun in this passage represents God. And the woman clothed with the sun represents Christ's bride, or God's chosen people. (She's crowned with twelve stars, which stand for the twelve tribes of Israel, as well as the twelve disciples.) Finally, the child to be born here is Jesus, the deliverer. The passage continues:

"There appeared another

wonder in heaven; and behold a great red dragon [the devil] having seven heads and ten horns, and seven crowns upon his heads. And his tail drew the third part of the stars of heaven, and did cast them to the earth: and the dragon stood before the woman which was ready to be delivered, for to devour her child as soon as it was born" (verses 3-4).

Satan is pictured here as waiting on the earth to destroy the Christ child "as it was born." And oh, how often the devil tried to devour Jesus! Satan first used Herod to try to destroy Christ, ordering the evil king to murder all the male babies in Bethlehem. Herod's "exceeding anger" was a demonic rage —an incarnation of the devil himself!

You might wonder, "If Herod was Satan-possessed, why didn't the devil point out to him which child was Christ? Why did all male babies have to be killed?" The Lord blinded Satan's eyes! As this passage tells us, God hid Christ from the enemy for a season: "She brought forth a man child, who was to rule all nations with a rod of iron: and her child was caught up unto God, and to his throne" (verse 5).

Next, scripture says, "There was war in heaven: Michael and his angels fought against the dragon; and the dragon fought and his angels, and prevailed not..." (verses 7-8). This war was waged by Satan against the son of God —and the devil lost. He was overcome by the blood of the cross —defeated once and for all!

Moreover, Satan lost his access to heaven: "...neither was their place found any more in heaven" (verse 8). "...that old serpent, called the Devil, and Satan, which deceiveth the whole world: he was cast out into the earth, and his angels were cast out with him" (verse 9).

At one time the devil's movements weren't limited to the earth. Job tells us, "There was a day when the sons of God came to present themselves before the Lord, and Satan came also among them" (Job 1:6). The devil must have come before God's throne frequently as the "accuser of the brethren."

But today Satan no longer has God's ear. He can't accuse God's children of anything anymore because Christ's blood has prevailed over all his lies! Jesus intercession for us now has nothing to do with refuting Satan's accusations. As far as God is concerned, the victory of the cross negated them all!

Satan may lie to you, giving you no rest from his accusations. But he can't accuse you to the heavenly father. He's been banned from heaven and all his accusations are meaningless!

THE WAR RAGES ON —AND IT'S BEING WAGED ON EARTH!

The great cosmic war is no longer between Christ and the devil. Jesus now sits safely with the heavenly father, well beyond Satan's reach. But the devil is still waging a war against Christ —by directing it against his seed!

"The dragon was wroth with the woman, and went to make war with the remnant of her seed, which keep the commandments of God, and have the testimony of Jesus Christ" (Revelation 12:17). The same fury and temptation that Satan aimed at Jesus in the wilderness now comes against all who would follow Christ!

Peter gives us this warning: "Be sober, be diligent, because your adversary the devil as a roaring lion walketh about seeking whom he may devour" (1 Peter 5:8). This doesn't mean the devil is hovering in the cosmos somewhere, giving orders to his demonic hosts. We just read that Satan was cast down to earth, when Christ defeated him at the cross. Thus, the devil's kingdom is limited to the here-and-now.

(The "spiritual wickedness in high places" Paul speaks of has to do with spiritual depravity in high government offices and backslidden church leadership. Paul is saying Satan's spirit is at work in many who occupy these influential positions.)

Contrary to the thinking of some Christians, Satan doesn't possess omnipotent power. He has been defeated by Jesus and stripped of all authority. Nor is Satan omniscient —meaning he can't read minds. And he's not omnipresent —he can't be everywhere at one time. He is physically limited to being in one place at any one time.

But Satan does have principalities and powers stationed throughout the earth. And his host of demons feed him intelligence at his beck and call. They hear you when you pray, and they see your obedience to God. And that's what stirs up Satan's wrath against you!

When scripture says, "...(the devil) knoweth that he hath but a short time" (verse 12), it's not referring to the time Satan has left before the return of Christ. Rather, it's about continual deadlines —a series of short times the devil has to accomplish his work. It's all about the brief times he has to make war against God's saints!

As we examine what it means for the devil to have this "short time," we need to ask: What do we do that so angers him toward us? What causes him to flood us with hell's entire arsenal? How do we awaken the powers of darkness that try to devour us?

I believe we do three things that draw the devil's wrath:

1. WE ANGER SATAN WITH EVERY DEEP STIRRING TOWARD GOD!

Perhaps you've recently renewed your commitment to pray with all diligence. Or, maybe you've expressed a hunger to walk before the Lord in holiness. Or, perhaps you've consecrated your mind and body to God as a living sacrifice. You've cried out, "I'm not going halfway anymore. I'm giving everything I have to Jesus!"

These kinds of commitments stir up the devil's wrath as nothing else does. He knows that anyone whose life is wholly given to God is a great threat to his kingdom. He remembers the lives of Peter, Paul, Philip —individuals who stepped out of the crowd and cried, "I'm doing it God's way!" They surrendered all to Christ —and they wrought havoc on Satan's kingdom!

The devil knows all too well that everyone who seeks God with all his heart will find him...that praying saints will eventually prevail... that God will accept every living sacrifice given with a whole heart... that the hungry spirit will be satisfied.

But Satan also knows there's a period between the time the prayer is spoken and when it's answered. Beloved, that is the devil's "short time" to work! He knows the "importunate widow" cried for a season before she was heard. And, likewise, our answer will come in due season. In the meantime, the devil tries to devour us, as we wait on the Lord!

The fact is, God doesn't jump every time we cry, "Lord, I give it all to you!" God knows that consecration, surrender and hunger for Christ don't always accompany a one-time, emotional cry. Therefore, his Spirit doesn't respond until he sees in us a sustained determination —some kind of evidence that we won't turn back from our hunger. Satan recognizes this also. He knows from having observed our lives when we're not serious about our commitment to the Lord. If we're not serious about following through, he doesn't waste his time on us. He leaves us alone in our weakness and sin.

But the moment he sees true devotion in us —a desire to be set free from sin, a determination to put off all foolishness and put on Christ —then he knows his time is short. He knows there will be only a brief period before we're out of his clutches and walking in glory, operating by faith, living in victory. That's when he starts throwing everything in hell at us!

This is the very reason why so many dedicated believers in the body of Christ are going through intense trials right now. Revelation 12 is telling us: "Go ahead, Christian -- step out of your lethargy. Yield your body to Jesus as a living sacrifice. Trust the Holy Ghost to deliver you from every lust. Seek God with all that's in you. But be prepared to face the trial of your life —because Satan will come at you with all his might!"

"The serpent cast out of his mouth water as a flood after the woman, that he might cause her to be carried away of the flood" (Revelation 12:15). You're going to be inundated with awful temptations, harassing spirits, weariness, despondency, unbelief, discouragement. The enemy will try to afflict you in body, mind and spirit!

Satan knows your weak spots —your struggles with flesh, lust or mind problems —and he'll work hard on you in those areas. He'll try to carry you away in a flood of trials and temptations, doing ev-

erything he can to bring you down. He's frantic —because he sees you on the brink of victory, and he knows his time is short!

Tragically, the devil often succeeds in this "short time." Many believers give up the fight, giving in to temptation and despair. They believe Satan's lies that they're no good, unclean, never going to be free. And they end up shipwrecked in their faith.

Yet the truth is, such lies never reach God's ears. He won't allow anything of Satan in the heavens. So, we have to shut out the devil's lies as well, by faith in Christ's work on the cross!

2. ANOTHER DEADLINE OF THE DEVIL IMMEDIATELY FOLLOWS OUR OBEDIENCE TO A FRESH CALL TO SOME MINISTRY OR SERVICE.

Ask anyone who has been called by God to step out into some new work of the kingdom —and that person will tell you Satan has come at him in a rage, hurling one affliction after another.

The devil listens to you. He hears all about that new step of faith God has called you to take. You've prayed over it, you've talked about it, you've sought counsel from others for it. And when Satan heard you say yes to God, he knew he had but a short time to utterly destroy that call!

So it was in the life of Christ. No sooner was Jesus baptized -- with the dove appearing, and the voice from heaven declaring him the "lamb of God, the savior of the world" —than Satan went to work. He knew he had only forty days and nights to try to devour Jesus and stop his ministry. And he worked feverishly, using every ploy of hell!

No sooner did Jesus declare

Peter a rock of faith than Satan moved in to sift the disciple, driving him to unbelief and betrayal. Satan knew he had to act quickly in Peter's life, before Jesus words about the disciple could come to pass. But the temptation ultimately failed — because one day that rock of a man struck fear in Satan's kingdom!

I know what this kind of hellish attack is all about. I am just now emerging from one of the most painful experiences of my life. And it all happened because God recently put a fresh call to ministry on my life!

After spending much time in prayer, I have sensed God's call to expand my ministry by speaking to pastors around the world. (I am not leaving the ministry of Times Square Church, or the ministry of these written messages. I am only adding this occasional aspect of ministry, by the direction of the Holy Spirit.)

I plan to speak this spring to gatherings of pastors in four nations -- France, Romania, Poland, and Macedonia and the Balkans. This last gathering would include pastors from all the ethnic groups there that hate one another - Serbian pastors, Albanian pastors, pastors from Kosovo and the Balkan countries. These men would be worshipping together, standing as one in Christ, in love with him and one another.

Yet no sooner had I scheduled this trip than Satan moved in. Up to that point I had been at a peak of health. But suddenly I was struck down physically. Within a matter of hours I became so weak I could hardly walk. I felt sharp internal pains, as if I were trying to pass a kidney stone. Soon blotches appeared on my stomach.

A doctor friend told me I had shingles —a disease that comes from the remains of childhood chickenpox. The older you are when you get shingles (and I'm over sixty), the worse you feel it. I spent weeks in pain, and no medication could stop it. I developed sores on top of my blotches, and I couldn't sleep.

The devil seemed to be laughing, saying, "So —you're taking on this new ministry, are you? You won't if I can help it!"

Yet, right now, as I write this message within weeks of my trip, all the sores have disappeared. The Lord has raised me up and given me new strength. It all was warfare from hell!

It has always been this way, throughout my years in ministry. Every new acceptance of a call from the Lord has been followed by demonic attacks —particularly against my wife, Gwen, and my four children. The devil has often tried to scare me by threatening, "Every 'yes' to God will cost you your wife, your children, your health."

In the late 1980s, when we moved to New York City to establish Times Square Church, Gwen had another occurrence of breast cancer. She had to have an emergency operation, and afterward we wondered if the surgeons had gotten all the cancer. Then, on the day Gwen came home from the hospital, we received a call from Texas: Our daughter, Bonnie, was diagnosed with cancer. She had a 30 percent chance of survival.

I heard the devil laughing then, too, saying, "So, you think you're going to establish a church in New York? Think again, preacher!"

Satan tries to frighten and discourage every servant of God with such lies. Today Gwen is healthy and strong, and Bonnie has been clear of cancer for ten years. And right now, as I write this message, I feel no physical pain whatsoever.

The devil comes at us with these intense trials because he knows he has only a short time to try to destroy God's plans. But we are not to fear him!

John Knox is a great example of how we can face down the devil's lies. Knox was one of Britain's most powerful preachers. His awesome preaching caused kings and queens to tremble. And he lived a righteous life to back up the gospel he preached, uncompromising to the end.

In Knox's later years, when he became terminally ill, Satan faced another deadline. This man had angered hell probably as much as the apostle Paul had. So the devil set out, in the short time he had left, to send Knox into eternity in fear and unbelief.

Knox wrote, "All my life I have been tested and assaulted of Satan. But my present test has assailed me most fearfully. He has set to devour me, and make an end of me. Often, before, he would place all my sins before my eyes. He tried to ensnare me with the allurements of this world. But the Spirit broke those attacks.

"Now he has attacked me another way. This cunning devil has labored to persuade me that I have earned heaven by my faithfulness to my ministry!"

Knox knew that salvation came by faith alone. He had preached this all his life, stating clearly that no one can be saved by his own righteousness, no matter how many good works he'd done. But now Satan tried to damn the preacher by tripping him up over his own faithfulness!

Just before he died, Knox testified, "Blessed be God who has enabled me to beat down and quench this fiery dart by passages from the scripture. By the grace of God, I am what I am —not I, but the grace of God in me. Through Jesus Christ I have gained the victory. The tempter shall not touch me again in this short time. I will soon exchange this mortal life for blessed immortality through Jesus Christ!"

Thank God for the testimony of John Knox! He used scripture to stand against Satan, and the Lord delivered him. He went home to glory singing God's praises in faith!

3. THE DEVIL HAS A DEADLINE WITH THOSE WHO WOULD COME TO CHRIST TO BE SAVED AND DELIVERED FROM SATAN'S POWER!

What I'm about to say may offend you. But the Bible states it very clearly: If you're a slave to lust, living in sin, without the Spirit of Christ in you, you're a child of the devil himself. Jesus says, "Ye are of your father the devil, and the lusts of your father ye will do" (John 8:44). He's saying, "Satan is in control of your life. Therefore, your father isn't God, but the devil. You're part of the enemy's family, not the Lord's!"

Of course, Christ spoke these words to a religious crowd who thought they were good in God's eyes. They were outwardly clean and religious but inwardly they were full of lust, sensuality, fornication, covetousness.

Yet there is also a sickness that strikes the children of the devil. It's called "sin-sickness." The deeper in sin a person falls, the more critical this sickness becomes. It reaches its peak when sin suddenly loses its pleasure, becoming boring and unfulfilling.

Sin-sickness drove a famous young TV star to suicide just weeks ago. The actor was starring in a hit series and making a fortune. He had just signed contracts to star in movies and was dating a beautiful actress. He had fame, fortune and good health.

But then his lifeless body was found in a cheap porno hotel. Apparently, none of the world's pleasures had satisfied him. His life had become empty, meaningless —and suicide finally ended it all. He died as a result of sin-sickness!

If you've never given your life to Jesus, then up to now the devil has had complete control over you. He has ruled and reigned over your life. But perhaps now Satan sees a change coming over you — and he knows he's losing his hold on you!

Sin has suddenly lost its sweet taste to you. You don't go to the evil places you once frequented. And you're not as anxious to party anymore. Money no longer satisfies you, and neither do sex or possessions. You feel a growing emptiness inside you.

And now here you are, reading this message. Perhaps you've become willing to read the Bible. Nobody's making you do it; something inside is urging you to pick it up.

Dear one, right now Jesus is knocking at the door of your heart, and the devil knows it. And the one thing Satan fears most is that you'll open the door to Christ!

FROM THE MOMENT THE DEVIL HEARS THAT KNOCK ON THE DOOR OF YOUR HEART, UNTIL THE TIME YOU OPEN AND RECEIVE CHRIST, ALL OF HELL GOES INTO A PANIC!

The devil knows he has only a short time left to work on you. And now he's going to try everything he can to keep you from answering God's call! The gospel of Luke tells us of a father who brought his demon-possessed son to Jesus. Christ told the father, "Bring thy son hither. And as he was yet a coming, the devil threw

him down, and tare him" (Luke 9:41-42). The word "tare" here means "violently convulse, terribly shake."

This young man was coming to Christ —about to be set free, translated out of the kingdom of darkness and into the kingdom of light. The devil saw he was about to lose another victim. So, in a rage, he threw the young man to the ground in one last, violent attack. He wanted to kill him and take his soul before Jesus could deliver him!

Satan will try to do the same thing to you today. The moment you move toward Christ, he'll attempt one last devouring attack. He'll put before your eyes the most alluring temptations. He'll try to cast you down with lies, telling you you'll never be free from sin and lust. He'll try to convince you you'll always be his, not God's!

But let me remind you: The instant you move toward Jesus, the devil is rendered helpless. He can't stop anyone who's headed to Christ! He couldn't keep the demon-possessed young man from reaching Jesus. All Christ had to do was say a word: "And Jesus rebuked the unclean spirit, and healed the child, and delivered him again to his father" (verse 42).

James tells us, "Resist the devil, and he will flee from you" (James 4:7). So, how do you resist the enemy? You do it by faith alone! Simply come to Jesus, trusting he'll rescue you from Satan's clutches. "Whom resist steadfast in the faith" (1 Peter 5:9).

You can be free today. You can say to Satan, When I finish reading this message, I'm going to be a free person. Jesus is my savior —and he's going to deliver me from every lust and ungodly passion. It's all going to go because he said so!

The times ahead may get hard for you. But the father's glorious, blazing sun will shine ever

brighter for you!

—David Wilkerson died in 2011. He was the founding pastor of Times Square Church in New York City, where he ministered to gang members and drug addicts. In 1971, he founded World Challenge, Inc., which supports missionaries and outreaches throughout the world.

Reprinted by permission: World Challenge, Inc., PO Box 260, Lindale, TX 75771. http://worldchallenge.org

HOW TO FOLLOW GOD'S VOICE -- IN SPIRITUAL WARFARE

THE IMPORTANCE OF FASTING

Jesus and Fasting

1. Jesus fasted 40 days before confronting Satan.
   a. **Luke 4:1** "Jesus full of the Holy Spirit . . .."
   b. **Luke 4:14** "Jesus returned to Galilee in the power of the Spirit . . .."

From our Lord's example, fasting does not change our position with God. It intensifies the power released toward satanic powers and strongholds.

2. Jesus instructed us to fast.
   a. **Matthew 6:16–18** Jesus said "when," not "if."
   b. **Matthew 9:15** ". . . When the bridegroom will be taken from them; then they will fast."

"It is clear that Jesus expected believers to fast after he was gone. This age is the time of the "bridegroom's" absence, from the time of his ascension until his return. The Church awaits this return of the bridegroom. Therefore, fasting in this age is (1) a sign of the believer's longing for the Lord's return, (2) a preparation for Christ's coming, (3) a mourning of Christ's absence, and (4) a sign of sorrow for the sin and decay of the world" (*The Full Life Study Bible*, page 1422).

Fasting and the Early Church

After Jesus' ascension, the apostles often prayed and fasted—**Acts 13:2–3; Acts 14:23; 2 Corinthians 11:27.**

According to the Bible, God's people should fast.

When:	Who:	Scripture:
Under chastening	King David	**2 Samuel 12:16–23**
Under judgment	King Ahab	**1 Kings 21:27**
In need	City of Nineveh	**Jonah 3:5–9**
In danger	Esther	**Esther 4**
Worried	King Darius	**Daniel 6:18**
In trouble	Ship at sea	**Acts 27**
Desperate in prayer	Paul at conversion	**Acts 9:1–19**
In worship and prayer	Anna in the temple	**Luke 2:37**
Seeking understanding	Daniel	**Daniel 10**
Casting out demons	Jesus' disciples	**Mark 9:14–29**
Needing guidance	King Jehoshaphat	**2 Chronicles 20:2–4**

Key Principles of Fasting

1. "How often have we made earnest prayer to God for some specific need, with the assurance that this was in the will of God, and yet there has been no answer from heaven. Why? It could be, and often is, that God is saying to us, 'When you seek me with all your heart, I will be found by you' **(Jeremiah 29:13, 14).** When a man is willing to set aside the legitimate appetites of the body to concentrate on the work of praying, he is demonstrating that he means business, that he is seeking with all his heart, and will not let God go unless He answers" (*God's Chosen Fast*, p. 50).

2. "How can we expect the power to flow if we do not prepare the channels? Fasting is a God-appointed means for the flowing of His grace and power that we can afford to neglect no longer" (*God's Chosen Fast*, p. 32).

3. Fasting deals with two great barriers to the Holy Spirit erected by man's carnal nature: the stubborn self-will of the soul and the insistent self-gratifying appetites of the body. See **1 Corinthians 9:27** (". . . I beat my body and make it my slave. . ..") and **Galatians 5:17** (The sinful nature and Spirit are in conflict).

4. Fasting must be accompanied by prayer, time in the Bible and worship. Otherwise, Christians simply get hungry and weak, which is precisely what the enemy wants.

5. Methods of fasting vary and should be determined by health needs and God's direction. The degree of abstinence is not a measure of spirituality. Drink lots of water while fasting.

   Types of fasting could include: only liquids, bread and water, three simple meals including protein and carbohydrates, or abstaining from sugar or caffeine. The Scripture passages listed on the prior page mention different methods.

6. Don't let the father of lies **(John 8:44)** lie and rob you of the privilege and command of fasting.

Quotations from Arthur Wallis' *God's Chosen Fast* used with permission of David C. Cook. Quotations from the © 1992 *The Full Life Study Bible—NIV* used by permission of Life Publishers International, Springfield, Missouri, USA 65803.

LESSON 11

KEYS OF THE KINGDOM

MAIN PRINCIPLE

Is our prayer life self-centered or does it reflect God's heart? Prayer does change things. It can have an impact on our lives, families, cities, countries and other nations. We need to pray God's heart in all areas of our lives.

TEARING DOWN STRONGHOLDS THROUGH PRAISE

by Cindy Jacobs

AS WE COME BEFORE THE FATHER IN AN ATTITUDE OF INTERCESSORY PRAISE WE WILL SEE BREAKTHROUGHS WE MIGHT NEVER HAVE IMAGINED BEFORE.

It was the end of a powerful meeting for women. As the seminar came to a close, a woman came forward and requested prayer. Tears streamed down her face as she told of a serious problem with depression. She seemed on the verge of a nervous breakdown.

The ministers gathered around her. Though they prayed and prayed, there was no breakthrough. Recognizing the depth of the woman's problem, they called for someone to lead the group in intercessory praise -- praise warfare, as some call it.

As I played the piano, the group began warring against the works of Satan by worshiping the Lord. Rising to their feet, the women sang, clapped and shouted.

Suddenly the lady for whom they were praying began to weep. She said the cloud of oppression had lifted from her mind, and for the first time in years her thoughts were clear. How we rejoiced together at the goodness of God on her behalf!

Out primary motivation for worshiping God is that he is worthy of our praise and adoration. First and foremost, praise and worship delights the Lord and brings us into His presence, so He needs to be the focus of our attention. Yet as more and more Christians are discovering, praise and worship is also an effective weapon in our battle against demonic powers.

THE WEAPONS OF PRAISE WARFARE

I believe true intercession is twofold: One aspect is petitioning God for divine intervention on behalf of a person or group; the other is warring against the works of Satan. The incident when Israel prevailed over Amalek as long as Moses interceded might be considered an illustration of both aspects —petitioning and warfare.

The Bible illustrates many ways to incorporate praise with intercession in our prayer groups and personal prayer times. First, the Hebrew language has seven words for praise, which all can be used at different times.

Halal means to be boastful or excited; it represents a tremendous explosion of enthusiasm in the act of praising God (see Ps. 117:1). Jewish tradition relates this to the overthrow of the wicked.

Yadah means to thank, to give public acknowledgment to, to extend the hand, to worship with raised hands (see 2 Chr. 20:19-21).

Barak means to bless, to bow, to kneel in adoration (see Ps. 103:1-2).

Zamar means to touch the string, to make music to God. This is a musical verb for praise.

Shabach means to speak well of in a high and befitting way, to address in a loud tone, to shout, to command triumph (see Ps. 117:1).

Tephillah means intercession for someone, supplication, a hymn (see Is. 56:7).

Towdah involves extending the hand in thanksgiving. It means to give the sacrifice of praise (see Ps. 50:23).

August 1993, Charisma

These seven words provide us with a variety of praise activities that honor the Lord, bring us into His presence and release His power in intercession. But there's much more.

Walking and marching. God told Joshua: "Every place that the sole of your foot will tread upon I have given you, as I said to Moses" (Josh. 1:3, NKJV).

The march that Joshua and his troops made around Jericho was a type of intercession. In particular, it illustrates the importance of persistence in intercession. How many of us have stopped praying when only one more time around "Jericho" would have brought a breakthrough in our circumstances?

This type of marching produces deliverance today just as it did for the Israelites A man named Rick went to a prayer meeting that Joy Towe was holding in Dallas, Texas. Rick was a television producer with a big problem. He had a job lined up and no television equipment, and none he could rent.

Joy put Rick in the middle of their circle, and they marched around him after seeking the Lord in prayer. In Rick's words, "We pursued aggressively with warfare -- we were militant!"

After Rick left the meeting, he ran into someone from a TV production company who was looking for a manager. They had the equipment and the offices he needed. He ended up making money for them as well as meeting his own need.

Treading. "Through God we will do valiantly, for it is He who shall tread down our enemies" (Ps. 108:13). "Behold, I give you the authority to trample [tread] on serpents and scorpions, and over all the power of the enemy, and nothing shall by any means hurt you" (Luke 10:19).

Treading is very much like marching -- only more aggressive. Whereas marching sets boundaries in prayer, treading includes actually stopping the power of your enemy.

Singing. "You shall have a song as in the night…The Lord will cause His glorious voice to be heard, and show the descent of His arm, with the indignation of His anger and the flame of a devouring fire, with scattering, tempest, and hailstones" (Is. 30:29-30).

Our son, Daniel, was born with a clubfoot; it would not flex. The doctor said that he could not bend it forward and, therefore, would not be able to walk well. One night, as I held Daniel, a chorus came to my heart:

"The devil had me bound, but Jesus set me free."

LAUGHTER IS AN IMPORTANT SAFEGUARD AGAINST HEAVINESS IN INTERCESSION. IT BREAKS SATAN'S POWER TO DEPRESS YOU IN THE MIDST OF BATTLE

I sang it over and over for an hour and then put Daniel to bed. The next morning while changing his diaper I noticed that his foot was flexible. His little shoe went on easily. Something happened to his foot when I sang over Daniel —the power of the enemy was broken, and God touched his foot.

Clapping. "Oh, clap your hands, all you peoples! Shout to God with the voice of triumph!" (Ps. 47:1). The word *clap* in this passage is teqae: to clang, smite, strike.

Nahum 3:19 exemplifies how *teqae* relates to triumph over enemies: "Your injury has no healing, your wound is severe. All who hear news of you will clap their hands over you." Clapping in the Bible is associated not only with praise but also with triumph in warfare. Clapping is one means of breaking yokes.

Shouting. "And the seventh time it happened, when the priests blew the trumpets, that Joshua said to the people: 'Shout, for the Lord has given you the city!' " (Josh. 6:16).

Shouting also can be an important aspect of praise warfare. What would have happened if the people circling Jericho had not shouted? Perhaps the walls would not have fallen down, and victory would not have been won.

Laughter. The weapon of laughter is extremely powerful and even necessary as an intercessory manifestation. As intercessors, we often hear many serious problems and needs during a day that can wear us down. But laughter is an important safeguard against heaviness in intercession. As Proverbs 15:13 says, "A merry heart makes a cheerful countenance, but by sorrow of the heart the spirit is broken."

What does laughter have to do with intercessory praise? It breaks Satan's power to depress you and oppress you in the midst of battle. Depression dilutes your spiritual strength. Medical studies have shown how laughter works like medicine. Deep laughter oxygenates the blood and causes positive physical changes.

Laughter also can be a form of direct warfare against Satan and his forces because it mocks the enemy. Psalm 37:12-13 says: "The wicked plots against the just, and gnashes at him with his teeth. The Lord laughs at him, for He sees that his day is coming."

August 1993, Charisma

Joy. Laughter and joy often are interrelated in intercession. Joy is an important part of our intercession because it is our strength for battle. Psalm 149:2 says: "Let Israel rejoice in their Maker; let the children of Zion be joyful in their King."

In her book *Praise Is,* Joy Towe says "the Hebrew word for *joyful* in this passage is *guwl,* meaning to spin around (under the influence of a very violent emotion)." Somehow our idea of joy is not the same as that. We are much more familiar with the quiet joy that is with us in our everyday walk with the Lord. The joy that comes in intercession, however, can run the gamut from laughter to violent emotion to quiet peace.

Joy in intercession can include jumping, leaping and rejoicing. It is often manifested as a dance. To our Western culture this may seem strange, but it is not at all strange in the Jewish culture, which is full of dancing in which the people spin, leap and rejoice.

SOME PRACTICAL APPLICATIONS

How can you include intercessory praise in prayer meetings? One of the first things to remember is that the Holy Spirit has many moods and ways by which He manifests Himself. To know how we should intercede, we need to maintain a sensitivity to His desires.

Another thing to consider is that the Lord works within our culture and often within our belief systems. Don't try to force any type of intercession. Let God establish it in your group. What might be appropriate in one church might be greatly out of order in another church.

How do these different types of intercessory praise come together? Here is one possible framework revolving around worship in an intercessory meeting.

It is good to begin with worship because many people come to prayer with heavy hearts. Jesus said: "Take My yoke upon you and learn from Me, for I am gentle and lowly in heart, and you will find rest for your souls. For My yoke is easy and My burden is light" (Matt. 11:29-30).

As we worship the Lord He will place on us His yoke, or His burdens for prayer, rather than our own. Many people are truly unable to intercede for the needs on God's agenda because they are too caught up with their own problems. They end up praying out of their emotions rather than by the Holy Spirit. But Matthew 6:33 exhorts us to "seek first the kingdom of God and His righteousness, and all these things shall be added to you."

It is often good to begin the worship with singing. Some will use hymns and others more contemporary choruses. Either way this is a good opener for your prayer meetings. Psalm 100:4 says: "Enter into His gates with thanksgiving, and into His courts with praise. Be thankful to Him, and bless His name."

Gates in the Old Testament were important places in cities. It was there that the elders sat to decide legal matters. The gates of the Lord are the places where His strategies are developed. As we begin our intercessory meetings with thanksgiving and praise, we open our hearts and minds to the revelation of His will.

During this time of worship consider the seven Hebrew words for praise we listed earlier. When God orchestrates our intercession the whole group will move together with the moods of the Holy Spirit. You might have, for instance, a time of *barak* when you adore Him silently. Other times you might lift your hands or clap.

You might then have a time of proclamation: "Violence shall no longer be heard in your land, neither wasting nor destruction within your borders; but you shall call your walls Salvation and your gates Praise" (Is. 60:18). Proclamation means calling out God's attributes —His names, character and nature.

Many times as a group worships together a song will come to someone's mind. The leader can determine whether the song is appropriate. It may be exactly what's needed to bless and comfort someone, to offer thanks to the Lord or to break the power of the enemy in the situation about which the group plans to petition. As you move into the intercession time, your group may use the other examples of intercessory praise discussed here.

You might all begin clapping, for instance. This is a hard, smiting type of clap. It is done with the intention of stopping Satan's devices in the situation you are warring with. You will know that it is accomplished because everyone will just stop. The Holy Spirit is the divine orchestrator. It is amazing how this happens.

TREADING ON FINANCIAL PROBLEMS

In some instances you might march over a tough case or actually put your feet down hard or tread. We used this kind of warfare at the North American Renewal Congress in Indianapolis in August 1990. The group was in prayer at 1 a.m. when one of the leaders of the renewal congress came into the prayer room. He explained that the congress was in serious financial jeopardy. They needed a $300,000 miracle by the end of the next day.

One intercessor pulled some money out of his pocket. People

August 1993, Charisma

who had very little gave sacrificially. One Catholic nun who worked in a leprosarium and lives by faith gave all she had.

When the money was piled on the floor, we began to pray with intercessory praise. We knelt and adored the Lord (*barak*), thanking Him for His provision. We wrote Satan a message and taped it to the bottom of our shoes! We let him know that he would not put the renewal congress in debt and cause a blight to come on the name of that organization. Then the intercessors trod upon the enemy. We marched and rejoiced in God for His provision.

The next evening the final session closed and people were starting to leave. The offering taken that night totaled $150,000 —a great amount but $150,000 short. Some of us were standing around the platform when a small, unassuming woman came up to Vinson Synan, president of the group. "Excuse me," she said, "but I would like to know how much the deficit is." Dr. Synan told her that it was $150,000. She then said, "I would like to pick up the deficit. I will have my foundation send you a check next week." God had provided.

And He will continue to provide for us —for healing, assurance, financial needs, protection. As we learn more of His desires for us, and come before Him in an attitude of intercessory praise, we will see breakthroughs we might never have imagined before. Powerful tools are at our disposal. We need only learn from Him how to use them.

—Adapted from *Possessing the Gates of the Enemy* by Cindy Jacobs, copyright 1991. Published by Chosen Books, a division of Fleming H. Revell Co., Tarrytown, New York.

Cindy Jacobs is a respected prophet who travels the world ministering not only to crowds of people, but also to heads of nations. Cindy has authored several197 books, including *Possessing the Gates of the Enemy, The Voice of God* and *The Power of Persistent Prayer.* Cindy loves to travel and speak, but one of her favorite pastimes is spending time with her husband Mike, two grown children and their adorable grandchildren.

Reprinted by permission Charisma Magazine and Strang Communications Company.

LESSON 12

VICTORY

MAIN PRINCIPLE

If we plan to be used by God to advance His kingdom, we will definitely feel the enemy's resistance. However, we have been given offensive weapons that counteract the tactics of the enemy. We will see victory when we remember that "spiritual warfare is not just a prayer prayed or a demon rebuked—it is a life lived."

ASSIGNED ARTICLE

SPIRITUAL WARFARE THROUGH WORSHIP

by Greg Mira

The subject of spiritual warfare is receiving great attention in the Body of Christ around the world right now. Books are being written and seminars are being taught, all with a view to help Christians gain a better understanding of how to "wage war" on the kingdom of darkness.

While I do not think that most believers would disagree with the concept of spiritual warfare, I do think there is great disagreement over how we should approach the battle.

I believe that the subject of spiritual warfare might well become one of the great "new controversies" facing the church in this hour. The argument will not be over the fact of spiritual warfare but rather the methodology of it. There are already rumblings coming from various camps that are beginning to draw lines around what they perceive to be "Biblically accurate" approaches to the conflict. Is it not interesting that the debate about spiritual warfare might become something our adversary uses to keep us busy fighting each other, over the details of how we are to be fighting him?

I must confess that I do not completely understand all about the tactics of spiritual combat or the rules of this war. I am not sure that anyone does right now. I do not think that this is the hour for any of us to be too dogmatic or arrogant about what we think we know. It is time for all of us to get low before God, walk humbly, remove our shoes and wait for the Captain of the armies of the Lord of Hosts to issue His battle directives.

I do believe that we have been summoned to get involved in the clash and to take part in it at a significant level of spiritual violence (Matt. 11:12). Ephesians 3:10,11 tells us that it is God's desire to demonstrate to the despotic rulers of this dark age His manifold wisdom. His intention is to use the church to accomplish this. In other words, the church has been called to minister to principalities and powers, but if we do not learn anything about spiritual warfare and never avail ourselves of the weapons at our disposal, they will not get the kind of ministry they deserve.

I want to be involved in the fight, and while I loathe the thought of God's people retreating, of allowing passivity to keep them idle, I believe that some of what we have called spiritual warfare borders on fellowship with the devil. What I mean by this is that much of our time, energy and spiritual resources may be focused in the wrong direction. If we are not careful and wise, we may end up giving so much attention and recognition to the powers of evil that we lose sight of the fact that it is Jesus, who already spoiled principalities and powers and made a show of them openly, who should occupy the position of preeminence and adoration in our midst.

> I BELIEVE THAT SOME OF WHAT WE HAVE CALLED SPIRITUAL WARFARE BORDERS ON FELLOWSHIP WITH THE DEVIL.

My point of concern here has to do with the focus of our strategy. Should our focus be "God-centered" (i.e. being taken up with His Glory, power, character, dominion, etc.) or should our attention be fixed on the spirits of darkness themselves (i.e. directly addressing certain "named" or unnamed spirits, "binding" the strong man, etc.)?

It would seem to me that there is ample evidence in scripture that the primary focus of our attention should be directed toward the one who really has the power to deal effectively with these demonic forces. The one who is the Lord, the Lord strong and mighty in battle (Ps. 24). When God shows up, His enemies scatter (Ps 68:1). The speed of darkness is 186,000 miles per second—right ahead of the Light. Light drives out darkness. What we need is the presence of God, not irresponsible diatribe or railing denunciations about things we do not completely understand (Jude 8-10). We are not to be overcome by evil, but we are to overcome evil with good (Rom. 12:21).

There are 25 apostolic prayers offered in the New Testament. Not one records a request for the removal of darkness or evil, but for a release of light and an impartation of good. I am not saying that we could not or should not ask God to do this. All I am saying is we must not allow our focus to be drawn away from Jesus and to be turned toward vile beings who clamor for our attention. Why curse the darkness when you can light a candle?

Two of the greatest weapons that God has given us for fighting against the powers of darkness are worship and intercession. Paul speaks in II Corinthians 6:7 about having weapons of righteousness in the right hand and in the left. The elders in Revelations 5:8 are seen holding a harp (worship) in one hand and a golden bowl of incense (prayer) in the other. There is no question that our worship can become one of the preeminent means of inflicting galactic mayhem on demonic activity (Ps. 149).

The problem I see in some instances, however, is that this type of warfare is generally only thought to happen when we sing the ever

popular…rock 'em sock 'em!, turn up the volume!, devil come out or I'm comin' in after you! "fight songs."

Now do not get me wrong. I love those songs too! I am just trying to say that we are greatly deceived if we think that volume, beat, words or banners are going to intimidate the devil. They do not! What does frighten the devil are lives that are being lived out in righteousness and true holiness—mixed with worship. That scares the devil out of the devil!

If our lives and lifestyles do not reflect a sincere commitment to obedience and purity, then the words we say or the songs we sing will not have any serious effect on hell. Acts 19:13-16 shows us that evil spirits are able to recognize the difference between true spiritual authority and religious hype. All of the "war songs" in our arsenal will not drive away the enemy if he knows that we are just going through the mechanics of a worship service or making superfluous declarations without a willingness to lay down our lives and take up our cross.

Revelation 12:11 says: *And they over came him because of the blood of the Lamb and because of the word of their testimony, and they did not love their life even to death.* Our testimony must match our manner of life. If we expect to experience true apostolic power, we must be willing to embrace a truly apostolic lifestyle. That means we are ready to worship God in truth as well as in Spirit. While trying to worship God in truth alone may be branded legalism, attempting to worship Him in Spirit alone is mere fanaticism. We must have both!

In II Corinthians 10:3-5, the apostle Paul talks to us about spiritual war and how to fight it. He then goes on to say in verse six that every

act of rebellion and disobedience will only be reproved when our obedience is complete. How can we demand obedience and submission of anyone (demons included) when we ourselves refuse to fully submit our lives to the Lordship of Jesus? It could be a very dangerous thing for us to attempt to spar with the forces of darkness if there is anything in our lives that they might be able to get hold of (Job 41:8,9).

Jesus said in John 14:30 that the prince of darkness was coming, but there was nothing in Him that he would be able to "latch onto." The reason was because Jesus loved the Father and always did exactly what He commanded Him to do. What a wonderful thing it would be for us to be able to say, "He has nothing in me!"

I am simply trying to say that just because there is a shout in the camp does not assure us of victory (i.e. I Sam. 4:1-11).

Exodus 32:17,18 tells us that Joshua, Moses' young protege, heard a sound ascending from the Israelite camp and immediately interpreted what he heard as the sounds of war. Moses, the seasoned man of God, knew better. He responded by saying that it was not the sound of victory or the sound of defeat, but the sound of singing. I wonder how much of what some of us have labeled "warfare" is simply the sound of singing?

I do not believe that spiritual warfare is waged by using any particular kind or style of worship music. Rather, I believe real spiritual worship occurs when we come into God's presence with clean hands and a pure heart (which is the only way you will ever get there, by the way—Ps. 24:4), by offering up sacrifices "acceptable" to God, and then trusting God to come out strong against our enemies. Isaiah

30:32 says that *every blow of the rod of punishment, which the Lord will lay on him, will be with the music of tambourines and lyres; and in battles, brandishing weapons, He will fight them.*

We must remember that not only is the victory the Lord's, but the battle is as well (II Chron. 20:15).

——Greg Mira served as the senior pastor of Metro Vineyard Fellowship's Lee Summit Worship Center in Kansas City, Missouri. He has travelled extensively teaching on worship. His burden is to see the Body of Christ released in power through purity and praise. His blog, found at blog.gregmira.com, is a means to that end.

Reprinted with permission: Psalmist Magazine

THE UPPER ROOM PERFUME

by Scott Hagan

REVIVAL NOT ONLY BRINGS SALVATION AND DELIVERANCE, IT ALSO RESTORES A CHURCH'S GOOD NAME IN THE COMMUNITY.

JUDAS ISCARIOT SAT ON THE WALL, JUDAS ISCARIOT *had a great fall. All the king's horses and all the king's men couldn't put Judas together again!*

The graphic crash of Jerusalem's infamous landowner gave new meaning to the term "buyer's remorse." His death taught bluntly that money and materialism are no antidotes for guilt, that greed and grace are a lethal mix.

Watching him leave the Last Supper, fully engulfed in a spirit of treason, you wonder how Jesus maintained an appetite for lost souls. But tragically, this sorrowful script was nothing new.

> "SATAN ADORES THE STATISTICS OF THOSE WHO FALL AND FAIL. IT'S THE ONLY TRUTH THE DEVIL PREACHES."

For every Exodus from Egypt, history reminds us that there are also the bones of a dead Egyptian buried somewhere in the sand. For every wall of Jericho laid waste by God's wrecking ball, there's also an Achan with a dirty basement. And for every beheaded Goliath, there's a shapely Bathsheba caught in a king's adulterous web.

The glorious birth of the church in the book of Acts found no exception. For concurrent with the resplendent ascension of Christ on the Mount of Olives was the scandalous departure of Judas at *Akel Dama*, the Field of Blood.

Maybe a contemporary version of this ugly rerun recently aired in your town. Perhaps it went like this: The renowned pastor in a neighboring community sends his flock into shock by running away with the church receptionist.

Your head slowly moves from side to side. You knew this man. The serenity and innocence of your own ministry feels raped. Your lips mumble imperceptible commentaries. A critical spirit simmers. You always knew his cars were a little too shiny, and his hugs with the ladies a bit too tight. You conclude that his fake heart must have come in the same package with his fake hair.

Satan adores the statistics of those who fall and fail. It's the only truth the devil preaches.

Welcome to the very anguish that scorched Jerusalem with the rise and fall of Judas Iscariot, the spiritual forefather of Benedict Arnold. If Jesus had been executed by gunfire, Judas would have volunteered to stop at army surplus to buy the bullets; a hanging, he'd have the rope in the back of his pickup. Some even say that he left the Last Supper without paying his tab.

The Bible leaves little to the imagination when describing the grotesque ending to Judas' life: "He burst open in the middle and all his entrails gushed out" (Acts 1:18, NKJV). The gruesome death scene at the Field of Blood would have made any mortician blush.

But this was far more than another death certificate for the obituaries. This was a follower of Jesus, the guy who settled for a quick buck over a signature pillar in heaven. This was news. "And it became known to all those dwelling in Jerusalem" (Acts 1:19).

With the bare shins of the church exposed, hell took a mighty kick. A defeated but delighted Satan paraded the report of an AWOL disciple down the streets of Jerusalem like a New Year's Day float.

As the woeful news of Judas echoed throughout Jerusalem, it looked as if the early momentum from the resurrection would be derailed. The church had pulled a hamstring. It wasn't the start the disciples were looking for.

But while Satan was running extra copies of Judas' death story for the morning paper, an unexpected arsenal was brewing just above the rooftops of an upper room. It had fire, but not the smell of smoke. It was fragrant. God was about to thoroughly fumigate Jerusalem from the smell of Judas Iscariot.

Soon everyone would forget Judas. Forget his failure. Forget the painful damage. Sarcasm and scorn would turn to gasps as 3,000 guests gave their hearts to Christ during Peter's first service. The avalanche of new converts would erase the old news of an apostolic con man.

"Then those who gladly received [Peter's] word were baptized; and that day about three thousand souls were added…And they continued steadfastly in the apostles' doctrine and fellowship, in the breaking of bread, and in prayers" (Acts 2: 41-42).

By Acts 2, the city was gossiping about grace, chewing on the miraculous. But isn't that what revival is supposed to do?

Are the atheist vultures circling the skies above your church? Your resolution will never be found in argumentation, equal time or a rebuttal to the editor. You must overwhelm the past with a healthier dose of the present. There needs to be a new noise in your city -- a noise that starts in the heavens, pours through the roof, fills up the heart, then floods down your streets.

Satan tries to fill the church with the smell of death:

- the smell of immorality
- the smell of church splits
- the smell of personal tragedy

Jerusalem knew that smell. But the Holy Spirit filled the holy city with a new aroma. He dreams of doing the same for you.

There will always be a few smelly corpses of Christian failure for the church to step over. Some may even stink from coast to coast. The eulogy given by Dr. Luke, however, says it all. He reported that Judas *exploded* and was never heard from again.

At the same time, yet another explosion rocked Jerusalem. It was the detonation of the church on the day of Pentecost. It caused a sound so deafening, produced an aroma so sensational, that the odorous effects of Judas Iscariot's compromise were forever buried and forgotten.

Ah, take a deep breath. The delightful bouquet of revival is filling our atmosphere. It's time to elevate like an eagle and rise above the compost pile of the past. Yesterday is 6 feet under.

Now, let's get out there and "go tell it on the mountain"!

—Scott Hagan and his wife Karen are the founding pastors of Real Life Church in Sacramento, California. They have a thirst for Jesus and a love for the city of Sacramento. Scott has a passion for the outcast, as well as a passion to inspire growing leaders. He has authored *They Walked With the Savior* and *They Felt the Spirit's Touch.*

ZOE COURSE DESCRIPTIONS

"My sheep __hear__ My voice, and I __know__ them, and they __follow__ Me." John 10:27 (KJV)

HEARING COURSES

Hearing God's Voice

In this course, everyone is encouraged to participate by applying the principles they read in scripture in order to learn to recognize when the Holy Spirit is speaking. The inner knowing, inner voice, and the authoritative voice of the Holy Spirit are discussed, as well as other manifestations of the Holy Spirit. The Lord is personal and unique, and desires to communicate with each one of His sheep in a personal and unique manner! (This course is a prerequisite for all the following courses except for How to Hear God's Voice —In Marriage.)

How To Hear God's Voice—In Christ

In the Hearing God's Voice course we learned how to hear God as individuals, whereas in the In Christ course, we learn how the body of Christ operates together under His direction and to His glory. We look at Romans 12 and examine the motive gifts that determine our individual bents. This study enables us to understand, appreciate and love each other. We also look at the Trinity and how they operate together. We learn about the precious person of the Holy Spirit and how He teaches, guides and comforts us. We also learn about the gifts of the Holy Spirit in 1 Corinthians 12 and 14 brought about as the Holy Spirit moves through us. Participants have remarked that this course has enabled them to see people the way God sees them and how they fit in the body of Christ.

How To Hear God's Voice—In Marriage

This course is based on the love relationship God had with mankind in the very beginning. We examine our attitudes toward each other and how they reflect the greatest love of all, the love of Christ. Do we love and honor each other with the unconditional love that our Lord Jesus had for us while dying on the cross? As in previous courses, we examine scripture, seek the Lord, and ask Him, "How can I better serve and love my spouse?" We discover how we complete each other, not compete with each other.

How To Hear God's Voice—In the Family

In today's society we see the growing deterioration of the family. Parents are confused about what the Bible teaches on family issues. During this course we examine scriptures and what it means to: "Train up a child [early childhood] in the way he should go [and in keeping with his individual bent], and when he is old [teen years can be the best] he will not depart from it." (AMP with additions)

KNOWING COURSES

How To Know God's Voice—In Intimate Friendship

Intimate Friendship with God! Can we experience such a relationship with the Creator of the universe? Here we examine what the Bible teaches us about the fear of the Lord, and how we can, indeed, have a deeper, more intimate relationship with Him. This is a very personal, yet freeing course on growing intimacy with God.

How To Know God's Voice—In Worship

The focus of this course is on ministering to the Lord. During our time together the Lord draws us corporately into His presence as we worship Him. We study what worship is, why we worship, and how we worship.

How To Know God's Voice—In His Presence

The Lord is calling each one of His sheep to come into His presence and to know Him in a deeper way. This course is not for the new believer nor the faint in heart. Those who are serious about knowing the Father in a more intimate way will find this course challenging but rewarding. Examining Jesus' last days on earth will direct us into the presence of the Lord. This course is for those who have completed other ZOE courses.

How To Know God's Voice—In the Coming of the Lord

Many are proclaiming dates and times when the Lord Jesus will return for His bride. This course is designed to focus on our preparation for His coming, not when He is coming, and to better understand the Lord's statement of Revelation 22:20: "Yes, I am coming." It is the goal of this course to prepare ourselves as the bride of Christ, with hearts that will respond with "Amen. Come, Lord Jesus."

FOLLOWING COURSES

How To Follow God's Voice—In Healing

During this course we examine the scriptures in which Jesus healed the sick. The Holy Spirit highlights these passages as we study, and our faith increases! We realize that Jesus is the Healer, and we are simply His vessels as we listen to and follow His voice.

How To Follow God's Voice—In Power

Evangelism is often thought of as a bad word! In this course we come to realize that God has a special plan for evangelism for us if we are only sensitive and obedient to His voice. Preparing your testimony, leading someone in salvation, and discipling others are a few of the topics discussed in this course. This is a real life-changer as we minister in "power evangelism!"

How To Follow God's Voice—In Intercession

Jesus is in constant intercession (Hebrews 7:25). As we come before Him in worship, intercession is a natural outflow of our relationship with Him. By yielding to the Holy Spirit, our ministry to others through intercession will increase.

How To Follow God's Voice—In Spiritual Warfare

As we come to know and recognize who our Lord is, He reveals to us who He is not! The tactics of Satan and our spiritual weapons are defined in this course. The Lord leads us in spiritual warfare as He enlists and mobilizes His army!

ONE-ON-ONE DISCIPLESHIP

Discipleship by the Word of God and the Power of the Holy Spirit

This 12-week course was developed by a disciple-maker after many years of successful one-on-one discipleship. Through this method the Holy Spirit is allowed to minister to the disciple through the Word and the encouragement of the disciple-maker. No other techniques or methods are used.

The entire course has been designed to enable individuals to feel confident in making disciples as directed by our Lord: *"Therefore go and make disciples of all nations …."* Matthew 28:19.

Not only do the participants learn what discipleship means according to the Word of God, but they are encouraged to participate in a one-on-one discipleship program as part of the course. This training allows individuals to take great strides in their personal relationship with God and in ministry. It changes lives in a very simple, yet powerful way.

EVANGELISTIC OUTREACH — MINISTRY IN HOMES

Captivated by Their Character

This series of courses called Captivated by Their Character is designed to reach the unbeliever, new believer, and those needing a refresher course on the Trinity.

They are offered in a non-threatening, home atmosphere where every effort is made to make the participant feel comfortable with the material. For example, everyone uses the same Bible, referring to page numbers rather than books, no reading is required outside of the course, and they are given the freedom to express their inadequacies as a believer or non-believer.

The three 6-week courses inside Captivated by their Character are titled Who Is Jesus?, Who Is God the Father? and Who Is the Holy Spirit?, and are also bound separately.

Additional information is available on the ZOE website at www.zoeministries.org/zoe-courses

HOW TO FOLLOW GOD'S VOICE - IN SPIRITUAL WARFARE — MAGAZINE LIST

For your convenience we have included the following list of magazines from which this course's articles have been drawn. If you wish to receive these magazines on a regular basis, the subscription information below will help.

Charisma and Christian Life
Subscription Service Department
P.O. Box 420234
Palm Coast, FL 32142-0234

(800) 829-3346
www.charismamag.com

Christ For the Nations
P.O. Box 769000
Dallas, TX 75376-9000

(800) 933-CFNI
www.cfni.org

Ministry Today
(formerly *Ministries Today*)
Magazine Customer Service
600 Rinehart Road
Lake Mary, FL 32746

(407) 333-0600
www.ministrytodaymag

Psalmist
(formerly published by Kent Henry Ministries)
(636) 532-7711

www.kenthenry.com

Times Square Church Pulpit Series
c/o World Challenge
P.O. Box 260
Lindale, TX 75771

(903) 963-8626
www.worldchallenge.org/en/pulpit_series_newsletter
www.tscpulpitseries.org

www.ingramcontent.com/pod-product-compliance
Lightning Source LLC
Chambersburg PA
CBHW081151090426
42736CB00017B/3276